THE CHEMIST AND THE TECHNICIAN

BY SHELDON E. & UVA GILLESPIE FREY

Order this book online at www.trafford.com
or email orders@trafford.com

Most Trafford titles are also available at major online book retailers.

Print information available on the last page.

ISBN: 978-1-4120-6934-2 (sc)

Trafford rev. 04/03/2024

North America & international
toll-free: 844-688-6899 (USA & Canada)
fax: 812 355 4082

Dedication and Acknowledgements

We dedicate this book to all of our ancestors, family and loved ones who made our journey through life a memorable one.

We acknowledge the patience of our family, our publishers and any others impacted by our initial publication. We give special thanks to our daughter Lisa who has bridged the gap from rough draft to a final format for the publishers.

Thanks also goes to our niece Elaine Frey for supplying some

otherwise

missing

details. For

final

editing we

appreciate

the efforts

of our son-

in-law,

John Roy

Fisher and

Bonnie

Justice. For moments of inspiration, we thank our Lord.

TABLE OF CONTENTS

TABLE OF CONTENTS

TABLE OF CONTENTS

TABLE OF CONTENTS

TABLE OF PICTURES

TABLE OF PICTURES

TABLE OF PICTURES

TABLE OF PICTURES

ix

PREFACE BY AUTHORS

We, the authors, wanted you to know

Some details of how we lived and did grow.

Of course as you will soon see

It may have involved both you and me.

How could we tell of yesteryear

Without ringing in those relatives dear

But when the final lines were spoken well

Only the surface was scratched to tell.

Highlights we remember and chose to say

How things were then but not today.

We tried to speak ill of no one

And if your name is found well done.

If you find it not remember well

There is a story you might tell

To clear the air of wrongs we may have done

In citing our tales of life, love and fun

You can expand and tell us more you see

How you lived and grew a fine person to be.

Finally there is a most important thing

And a lesson to you we bring

We saw and felt so many times and places

The hand of the Lord and his graces

Some of these were hidden then

In retrospect, they appeared again and again

At turning points most obvious there

That we were in His constant care.

1 - In God's Country

What can one say or do?

When he comes to the scene anew?

O n April 29, 1921, my grandmother, Lucinda, helped to bring me to the light of day. Just before I was 4 years old I remember Lucinda's funeral because her coffin was in our house. Many doubt that I actually remember the coffin, but I do. She died of pneumonia in the spring of 1925.

More will be said of her later, but she was one of twenty children born to Joseph and Nancy Battin. In 1875 an old photo shows her as 18 years old, the next to the youngest of 10 siblings who survived childhood. In her adult life she served the community as a midwife.

You see we lived in God's country, for in the mid 1800's Peter Armstrong, a theological fellow from Philadelphia, set about to establish Celestia as a community where Christians could spiritually prepare for Christ's return to Earth. Four square miles were deeded to the Lord. Peter died in 1880 and Celestia disintegrated. The Lord did not pay "His taxes," so eventually the land was sold. This is a matter of record in Sullivan County, Pennsylvania, a county which today has but one traffic light.

I was not the oldest in our family for Dorothy was born in 1914, Kenneth in 1916 and Lawrence in 1918 who always challenged my earliest memory. He said do you remember my retrieving you from under the sofa so that grandma could "discipline" you. Other siblings included Alice in 1924, Irene in 1926 and Wayne in 1934.

I believe as early as I could handle firewood, it became my responsibility to supply the "Home Comfort" kitchen stove and the heating stove in the living room. On those bitter winter nights it was not uncommon to take a hot piece of wood from the kitchen oven wrapped in cloth as foot warmer on going to bed. You see the only heat we had upstairs was through a register mounted in the living room ceiling above the heating stove. Of course there was some loss of heat from the flue which went through the room. This home had no electricity and no indoor plumbing except for a cold-water tap to a sink in the kitchen.

2 - As Summer Fades

As the days do shorter grow
September is here you know.

September signaled the start of school with a new pair of bib jeans and a denim shirt from Sears Roebuck in Philadelphia. I will cover school in more detail in a later chapter. Fall was harvest time and many things came to mind, such as potatoes to dig and store. Potatoes which were used occasionally as a money crop with mixed results. Once during the early 30's, we planted 4 acres at $1.00 per bushel and harvested them at $0.30 per bushel. Another potato story is courtesy of Uncle Joe, one of Daddy's brothers. When he was a young man at home a customer objected to a peck of dug potatoes because of small potatoes. Uncle Joe removed the small potatoes and still had a peck. We had several apple trees some on the original 88 acres and then others on the additional 100 acres which

Daddy had purchased. These trees had not been pruned for years but they gave much fruit which shared separate storage in the unfinished basement. One year we traded a barrel of Northern Spy apples for a barrel of sweet potatoes with a mail order customer in North Carolina. Another year this trade did not prove economical.

Corn was harvested in shocks in the field until it was time for husking. Of course a few years later, corn was ground stalks and all and put in a silo as ensilage for cattle food. When the husking was done the ears of corn were placed in a corn crib near the pigpen. Butternuts were dried until the outside bark could be removed. The butternut tree was one that Daddy planted when he was a boy. Other vegetables such as cabbages, squash, potatoes, onions and beans were all gathered for fall and winter storage. It should be recognized that all summer long canning and preserving was a constant chore to provide for the winter's supply of food.

Before I fill you in on our household diet, I must explain about my father's father, John Frey (1854–1932). John Frey was born in the area around Easton, Pennsylvania. Cyrus, his father, came over with other German or "Pennsylvania Dutch" immigrants about 1825; apparently as an indentured servant. John's mother was Hannah. When a young man he told of a Halloween prank played on a victim. The pranksters had taken the farmer's wagon and mounted it straddling the peak of the barn roof.

The story that he sowed his wild oats and escaped the area of his birthplace apparently is true. What led him to travel to the northwest is unclear except that this forested area was soon to be harvested. He traveled the equivalent of three hours of today's auto drive before ending up in Sullivan County, Pennsylvania. Sullivan County was formed from Lycoming County in 1847 and is bounded on the north by Bradford, on the east by Wyoming and Luzerne, on the south by Columbia and Lycoming and on the west by Lycoming. He soon found the Battin family in Fox

Township, the westernmost of the county. Many years later Daddy and I were traveling along Elk creek before reaching the Hoagland branch when at a turn in the road he told this story. My grandfather had driven a team of oxen to Hillsgrove and was returning by the same route when the somewhat inebriated driver misguided his team and straddled a tree that stood on that curve. The story concluded that grandfather had to walk 5-6 miles because the oxen had escaped home ahead of him. There was no account of Joseph Battin's reaction.

John worked in tanneries at Grover and also in Hillsgrove (or Proctor). Daddy was born at Proctor (1/3/1889). Shortly after Lucinda's father died (1890) Lucinda used her inheritance to purchase the Peter Kilmer farm that became the Edwin Frey homestead.

John served on the school board and he was a Star Route Mail Carrier. My grandfather did very little work after Lucinda died in 1925. He died in 1932 in his favorite rocking chair. He had sung a "Pennsylvania Dutch" ditty that same morning. In his later years it was my job to see him to bed every night. This was done using a lantern and trying to make sure the bed covers did not weigh too heavily on his toes.

My grandfather demanded fresh fried potatoes every morning. To complete the meal there were usually eggs and always pancakes. Mother would vary the pancakes from wheat to corn to buckwheat. We grew our own buckwheat and had some ground for flour each year. Buckwheat pancakes seemed to be a favorite. One secret to having good buckwheat cakes is making the batter the night before. Syrup was usually made from brown sugar but on rare occasions maple syrup would be available. Bacon was also available on occasions since we usually had a hog to slaughter in the fall. The curing of pork was either by using salt and/or smoking.

While fried potatoes were standard for breakfast it usually would be boiled ones for lunch or supper. We never called our evening meal dinner. Other menu items would include beans and fresh or canned vegetables in season. I can remember salmon soup and crackers. I believe in those days you could buy quality salmon in a soup sized can for 10-20 cents a can. A standby favorite was "Johnny Cake" and milk on Saturday night. Johnny Cake was a corn-based bread. Then of course we might have fried corn mush on Sunday morning made from the solidified gruel from the night before. Mother baked all our bread and she would nearly have to fight us off when she did. Nothing tasted better than a freshly baked crust of bread with some butter.

One fall treat we had occasionally was chestnuts. As a teenager I remember 3 or 4 stately but dead chestnut trees, they having been killed by the chestnut blight. However, one tree in particular would keep pushing out new growth so that a few chestnuts could be enjoyed. Daddy recalled helping to harvest nine bushels one year when the trees were alive.

The fall season also presented the possibility of having squirrel and venison, though these weren't major items on our menu. Thanksgiving called for pumpkin pie and food aplenty but no turkey. The bird on the menu would be a roasted hen or two. I think my favorite piece was the drumstick if I could get it. At the end of the summer, I generally had gathered mints to dry which gave a rare wintry brew of spearmint, peppermint or pennyroyal. Boneset was collected which on rare occasions might be used as a poultice to draw the inflammation from a staff infection.

3 - A Sledding We Will Go

On winter's snow
A sledding we will go.

Winters vary as winters did. I can remember weather in the minus 20's and yet I can recall a neighbor plowing in January. You are probably curious about Christmas, we were too. Food menus were much like Thanksgiving ones. We generally received a box of fruit, nuts and candy from Uncle Joe and Aunt Sarah who were childless. Then Mother's sisters in Philadelphia might send something. I think if each child received something the day was big. As far as school was concerned we had one day off. Our Christmas tree was hemlock, our only local evergreen tree.

Sometime each winter when the ground was covered with packed snow there was a sledding opportunity. The sleds were usually ridden face down and forward except when riding a multiple bobsled. There was seldom any traffic so the roadways were used. Occasionally we had a condition where the snow was crusted and this presented a sledding variation for a grass-covered field. We had a short broad runner sled which I liked on crusted snow. Down the road about one-half mile was our nearest "ice rink." A muddy creek draining a swampy area was an attraction for beaver, and after a period of extended cold weather we tried our clamp-on skates and succeeded in brief periods of locomotion. It was not difficult to get wet which of course terminated the fun.

4 - Bluebird, Wren or Robin

The creek does flow

As we lose our snow.

With the coming of spring the song birds would return and the creek by the house would flow full. When summer came the stream would go dry from woodland to woodland. Spring was a time of considerable activity with much planting to be done.

Adjacent to the house on the western side was a favorite garden spot. It was covered with a good layer of barnyard manure and then plowed and well worked to provide a proper seed bed for the more sensitive vegetable seeds of carrots, onions, lettuce, beets, peas, radishes, etc. My recollection is that except for Mother's final year she was always able to work in this garden.

Gardens demanded weeding and hoeing and in short, tender loving care. While we grew several varieties of some vegetables, I can remember counting the vegetables and varieties one year and the total was about thirty.

One of Mother's many talents was her operation of a mini-nursery. Her key to starting plants as I see it was the previous sterilization of her planting media to prevent damping off. She did this by heat-treating the media first. She grew cabbage, cauliflower, tomato and pepper plants to sell to the community. In order to meet growing season demands these plants usually were started at home utilizing all available window sills.

As wild things started to grow, early greens included dandelions which were cooked and served with a bit of vinegar. Another item gathered were the early tender shoots of milkweed which made a novel green for the table. On occasions beautiful morel mushrooms could be found near the stream. Since Mother did not cook these I was able to obtain a few pennies from a neighbor who was glad to get them.

Spring saw the cutting and treating of seed potatoes against scab formation prior to planting. When possible, a good stand of sweet clover was plowed under in the preparation of the potato field. The sweet clover was planted the year before and it served to fix nitrogen in the soil which helped to promote the growth of the potatoes.

For dry beans a favorite procedure was to drop some dried chicken manure on the hill then cover it and plant the beans. Daddy often needed some help with spring plowing since his school-teaching duties usually did not end until early May. In addition to the garden area near the house there were two or three other areas for growing vegetables besides the potato field.

Crop rotation was the rule of the day to maintain food and crops for 6-10 cows, 2 horses, 2-3 pigs and a flock of chickens. A typical rotation could be after two years for hay a field would be used for corn then followed by oats with which one would reseed for hay again. Other crops included wheat and buckwheat as well as soy beans. The soy beans were used for supplemental cattle food in early summer.

5 - Good Old Summertime

How did you know
These things would grow?

The act of working a farm is to accept a goodly quantity of faith. Even when using your best techniques there was always some adversity, but rising above this generally produced results. Gardens needed weeding and hoeing in order to give the growing plants the best chance for survival.

As the corn grew, I would follow the cultivator to remove big weeds and to correct for minor cultivator mishaps. The same procedure was also used when the potatoes were hilled. Daddy had the ability of making straight rows that greatly facilitated the whole operation. Strawberries grew wild and were gathered and enjoyed or preserved for later use. Other berries that grew wild included red and black raspberries that were processed similar to strawberries. Blackberries were a joy to pick if one could avoid the thorns, because they were larger and your bucket filled faster. They were canned and used as such or enjoyed as part of a school lunch. Blueberries or huckleberries as we called them usually meant a trip to a nearby swamp where they grew in abundance. Peaches, cherries and grapes usually meant a trip to New York State where these were grown commercially. Whenever these fruits were obtained in quantity, especially peaches, they were processed for later use.

During the Roosevelt administration there were CCC camps near Hillsgrove and Masten. These Civilian Conservation Corps. men provided roads and firebreaks in the state forests. The man in charge of food purchasing welcomed the opportunity to buy fresh produce. I know that one summer we sold a good quantity of fresh produce to one of these camps. Green beans were one favorite I remember.

Cucumbers, tomatoes and other vegetables were enjoyed as they matured. The whole beet plants were served as greens when thinning was done in the garden. One of the

18

first farm crops harvested was soybeans or sowed corn which was cut as a green feed for the cattle. Hay or clover was cut and field-dried before bringing it to the barn for storage. Improper storage of hay could lead to spontaneous combustion and subsequent loss of property. Oats was grown for horses and buckwheat was a minor crop grown for chickens or milling for flour. Many years Daddy carefully planted about an acre of wheat in late summer. When this had matured the following summer, it was cut and stacked in round stacks and capped with two additional bundles.

Late in the summer a day was set aside for the use of a threshing machine to separate the grains from the straw. The straw was used as bedding for the cattle. In the case of the wheat, the grain was milled and the flour was stacked on the second floor until it was needed for baking. Also as needed a barrel of cider was also stored on the second floor. The cider was allowed to go to vinegar.

Speaking of cider, do you know the answer to this riddle? What is older than its "mother?"

6 - SCHOOLTIME

How was one to know

What to learn to grow?

My elementary school was one room with coat closets between the entry door and the classroom. The teacher would come early to build a fire and sweep the schoolhouse. Two outside toilets were on opposite sides of the schoolhouse. The ringing of the school bell at nine o'clock summoned about 30 children to meet. They were in grades one to eight. To start the day the teacher would read ten or more verses from the Bible and we would say the pledge of allegiance. For recitation each grade would in turn sit on a long bench at the front of the room. For example, the day would start with first grade arithmetic and proceed in order to the eighth grade that was followed by a recess time of about 15 minutes. A similar recess time would be held in the afternoon. The lunch-time break was an hour long.

Our South Street school yard was somewhat level but was ungraded. Besides the two outside structures there was a stack of wood for the Franklin stove. Typical games included tag around the schoolhouse, softball or in winter sledding was possible on the road by the schoolhouse. Some children were able to go home at lunchtime because they lived near by. The teacher maintained discipline by whipping the pupil when it was felt necessary. I remember a few punishments I received but by the time I was fourteen I should have known better than to make the teacher feel that I was impudent. I remember that being the end of my mistaken ways of behavior.

I have always considered that I was blessed by having the same teacher, Jesse Williams, for 6 of the 7 years that I was in grade school. Jesse, like my father, did some farming and on one occasion, perhaps my first, I spent the night with Jesse and Alma. One of the highlights of the evening was viewing a stamp collection that the teacher was maintaining. My old report cards indicate that midway through my first year I had started spelling class and I was promoted to the third grade for my second year in school.

All my siblings except Alice and me at sometime had our father as a school teacher.

During all Daddy's teaching experience he was obligated to take assignments on three occasions outside the township which had five elementary and one 2-3 year high school. One occasion that kept him away during the week was when he taught at Wylausing because of his religious affiliation at that time. Another occasion occurred when I was in third grade and he taught at Lincoln Falls. He took me to visit his school there on one occasion and I remember citing the "48 states" and their capitals starting from Maine and ending with California for one of his classes. I did this very quickly without assistance. As you see there was a benefit to the one room schoolhouse that was not immediately obvious. You had the advantage of hearing more advanced studies before you were at that grade level. For some playground disagreements I found myself protected since I was a note carrier. Some students gave me notes to give to my older siblings to deliver to some high school students and for this I had "protection."

At one time (1931-32) the Fox Township High School (3 years) was taught by two teachers. My brother Kenneth graduated in 1932 and then completed his fourth year at Estella by driving the family truck to school. By the time I went to this high school (1934-35, 1935-36) it was now a 2-year high school with one teacher. We had no foreign language classes so one year we had two math classes and the other year we had two history or social studies classes. I remember coming home from the county fair in 1936 and while passing through Estella I wondered what bus I would be on the next week.

Little did we dream of what was about to happen. Daddy's only sister lived in Canton and had phoned that William Watts (Murray's father) was looking for someone to help him with his custodial duties at Canton High School as well as the grade school located across the street from the high school. With a suitcase packed we made the trip to Canton and I became a household member of the Watts family, mother, father, daughter Frances and Murray. Murray had graduated from Temple University but was currently unemployed. As I started to learn my duties under Mr. Watts which even included the big furnaces which heated the school buildings, Mr. Watts suffered a heart attack and died. Murray was able to step into his father's assignment and so I was able to continue working. One change I will note was that I did not receive any further instructions with the big furnaces.

We generally arrived early in the morning in order to sweep out the rooms and hallways and gather the trash. Murray and I also had some additional help for some of the janitorial duties. It was planned that we would complete our work in the mornings or at noon so that the evenings would be free. For example, students with lunches would eat on the balcony surrounding the gymnasium. I would eat quickly because I immediately cleaned the lunch area. Following this, I would go to the grade school building, collect the trash, take it to the corner of the schoolyard and burn it. As the noontime ended I would unlock the doors of the elementary school to let the pupils return to their classrooms.

On Saturdays we would dust all erasers and wash all blackboards and do other chores that were not in the daily routine. Before school opening in the fall we would wash windows. Snow removal always presented an extra challenge.

Since I needed foreign language courses, I elected to take two years of Latin. I enrolled in the academic curriculum, while other choices were home economics, commercial or business and shop. Many of the teachers were new to Canton and a few of these later married and remained in Canton. Mr. Livesey was the coach and taught math as well. I remember his telling that the details we were learning would soon be forgotten but the logic and reasoning would be a lifetime companion. Miss Bunyan was in a class by herself. I took her chemistry course and later when I was enrolled in chemistry at Penn State I found that her fundamentals were excellent. I found that I was able to help students in chemistry who came from much larger schools.

My school grades at Canton as well as those from Fox Twp. served to make me valedictorian of the class of 1938 with its 67 members, which I recall was the largest class to date. My valedictory address attempted to say that our educational system was superior to those of totalitarian countries.

7 - ODDS & ENDS

We had fun along the way
But there is much more to say.

PROVERBS & VERSES

Many proverbs or verses became a part of me and lingered with me over the years and the authors of some of these are unknown.

"Tobacco is an Indian weed
And from the devil sprang the seed
It burns your pockets and your clothes
And makes a chimney of your nose."

- Unknown

"Lost, yesterday, somewhere between sunrise and sunset two golden hours each set with sixty diamond minutes, No reward is offered for they are gone forever."
  – Horace Mann

"Good, better, best
Never let it rest
Until your good is better
And your better is best."
  - Unknown

My father came back from a teacher's training and conference meeting one time with the following:

"In southern Pennsylvania the innkeeper's son was approached by the traveling salesman. The salesman said 'will you extricate the quadruped from the vehicle, stable him and donate him with an adequate supply of nutritious ailments and when the aurora of the morning again illuminates the oriental horizon I will award thee with a

pecuniary compensation for thy amiable hospitality.' The
boy ran to his father and announced that there was a
'Dutchman' who wanted to see him."

*"Lo, here hath been dawning another blue day: think, wilt thou
let it slip useless away? Out of eternity this new day is born,
into eternity at night it will return. Behold it aforetime no eye
ever did; so soon it forever from all eyes is hid. Here hath been
dawning another blue day; think, wilt thou let it slip useless
away?"*

> -- *Thomas Carlyle*

From a mural on the wall of the old Chemistry
building at Penn State there was the following.

*"Chemists are a strange class of mortals, impelled by an almost
insane desire to seek their pleasures amongst smoke and vapour,
soot and flames, poisons and poverty, yet amongst all these*

evils I seem to live so sweetly that I would rather die than change places with the King of Persia."

- Johann Becher, Physica subterranean, 1667

Then we have Alice Carey's great poem entitled Nobility that was much loved by my father and our family as a whole.

True worth is in being, not seeming,
In doing, each day that goes by,
Some little good -- not in dreaming
Of great things to do by and by.
For whatever men say in their blindness
And in spite of the fancies of youth,
There's nothing as kingly as kindness,
And nothing so royal as truth.

We get back our mete as we measure - -
We cannot do wrong and feel right,
Nor can we give pain and gain pleasure,

For justice avenges each slight.

The air for the wing of the sparrow,

The bush for the robin and wren,

But always the path that is narrow

And straight, for the children of men.

'Tis not in the pages of story

The heart of its ills to beguile,

Though he who makes courtship to glory

Gives all that he hath for her smile.

For when from her heights he has won her,

Alas! It is only to prove

That nothing's so sacred as honor,

And nothing so loyal as love!

We cannot make bargains for blisses,

Nor catch them like fishes in nets;

And sometime the thing our life misses

Helps more than the thing which it gets.

For good lieth not in pursuing,

Nor gaining of great nor of small,

But just in doing, and doing

As we would be done by, is all.

- Alice Carey

There were special days when relatives would come when Mother would put on a big meal. On the fourth of July we might have a picnic type meal. Home-made ice cream was a rarity I think because ice was not readily available. At the county fair you could buy a double dip cone for ten cents. The choices of flavors were limited to vanilla, chocolate, strawberry or maple walnut.

I did not do milking because Daddy, frequently Mother, Kenneth and Lawrence were there ahead of me. My chores involved the chickens, hogs and supplying wood for the kitchen and heating stoves. As the night fell I usually locked the chicken house, garage, and the corn crib when it was in use. I could sometimes hear the call of the "whip-poor-will" on these trips in the summertime. At one time we tried raising guinea pigs for medical research. All went well on the farm but the project failed because so many of the animals died of the heat during the shipment back during the summer months.

There were some disagreements between Kenneth and Lawrence at times. Kenneth enjoyed the privilege of driving to school as a senior in high school and I think this was part of the problem. Somewhat later when Kenneth and Marion were married on June 14, 1935, Lawrence chose to go fishing and I tagged along. He loved to fish but on this occasion it was mostly hiking for both of us. Little did Lawrence know that exactly six years later on June 14, 1941 he would marry Marion's sister, Leona. Dorothy kept the house clean and to a small degree Alice became her understudy. Irene loved to ride in the car and often she and I would quibble as to who would go with Daddy on this or that errand.

Shortly after Kenneth and Marion were married it was decided to tap a good stand of maple trees to make maple syrup. There was a lot of work involved in gathering the sap, boiling away the excess water and finishing off the maple syrup to the right consistency. Part of the fun came afterward, for if one concentrated the syrup a little further you could make candy or even taffy by pouring the syrup over clean snow or crushed ice. There were occasions to enjoy popped corn which was made in a covered skillet by moving it back and forth over the hot surface to keep the popcorn from burning.

My youngest brother was born in 1934 on Friday March 23 and everyone wanted to name him. Officially he was named Edwin Wayne Allen Frey but he grew up using the name Wayne. He was uncle the day before he was two years old as Mother and Daddy welcomed their first grandchild, Dolores.

Sullivan County had coal mining operations at Lopez/Mildred and Forksville during the early 1900's. The coal was not the anthracite type found in eastern Pennsylvania but tended to be more bituminous. The logging of timber had occurred at the same time or a little earlier. On the early maps of the township the post office was shown at Piatt. We knew this as a crumbling residence about a mile from Shunk. The first name for Shunk was Fox Center. The name Fox was in honor of George Fox, founder of the Society of Friends. The name Shunk was in honor of a former governor of Pennsylvania. Our address was Wheelerville through which the railroad was built.

In the early 1900's it was determined that if the Susquehanna and New York built a short line from Marsh Hill to Monroeton a considerable saving in the movement of freight could be obtained. Daddy played a minor role in this construction. During my early years the milk from Fox township was collected at Wheelerville and then shipped by rail. In its heyday I believe there were two trips each way each day on this rail line. Wheelerville had its general store as well as Shunk. During the second World War, this railroad was removed to supply iron for other purposes. Daddy once again played a minor role in its removal. Prior to the demise of the railroad the milk was trucked to Grover to a milk station at that location. In this transition period Wheelerville shrunk while Shunk grew, so today the post office is at Shunk. Sullivan County is known by some today as the county with only one traffic light, it is on Route 220 in Dushore, Pennsylvania. The population of Sullivan County has decreased every decade since 1910. For the most part residents do their significant shopping outside of the county usually in the nearest adjoining one. The real estate taxes are billed to residents and non-residents and the indication is that the billings are about the same for the two groups.

Our early church experiences were a bit complex because of the Quaker influence and Daddy's considerate attitude concerning the Seventh-day Adventists in the area. Over and above this was the Maple Summit church which at that time was a part of an Evangelical Lutheran pastorate. As I recall the minister would come every other week in the afternoon. As a teenager (13 and/or 14) I can remember playing the role of sexton where I had to build the fire and ring the bell for services. This trip from home through the woods was about one and one-half miles. On a winter's afternoon with a sled full of wood it was a slightly challenging trip. On the other hand the church at Shunk had no pastoral connection at that time. It did have a very active Sunday school service and Jesse Williams was the superintendent. In the summer of 1932 two evangelists came to the Shunk church and daytime classes were held as well as evening sermons. A number of us were taken to Canton where arrangements had been made for our baptism at the Baptist church. Later when I was in Canton on weekends I attended this church. So it was not uncommon to go to Shunk on Sunday mornings and to Maple Summit in the afternoon.

We had our ups and downs and the run of childhood diseases such as chicken pox, measles and mumps. The thing I remember about chicken pox was the terrible itching sensation which occurred at the onset on the disease. One time my sister, Alice, had a prolonged period of having a bad cough and when it was about to wear her out Daddy brought home some pineapple juice which helped to alleviate the condition. When I was about twelve my parents had trouble awakening me. They called the doctor who made the 10-mile trip and all turned out well with no particular reason given for the occurrence.

During the spring rains Daddy had placed a stone in the ditch of the road so Dorothy would not get her feet wet in crossing the road. On this spring day Lawrence, Kenneth and I were at the top of the hill along which the shortcut existed. Lawrence and Kenneth gave me a few yards start and I was to beat them home. On my way down, I stumbled a few feet from the road and fell on the rock in the ditch. To this day I carry a scar on my forehead where I connected with that rock. The spring rains were mentioned above and one of the pleasant sounds was going to bed during a rainstorm because with the rafters exposed upstairs the rain made its melody of bouncing just inches away on the roof.

One of the fields above and behind the house apparently was an old Indian camping ground since it was somewhat level and near an excellent source of water. The evidence for this was that nearly every time this field would be worked Daddy would find the flint arrow points so characteristic of the earlier inhabitants.

PEANUT BUTTER FUDGE RECIPES

Finally, I wish to remember the candy lovers of our family and maybe of yours, too. For peanut butter fudge you measure 4 cups of brown sugar into a medium saucepan and then add 1 and 1/3 cups of milk and carefully heat with some stirring and bring this mixture to boil. On boiling it is a good procedure to steam down the sides of the pan to remove any trace of crystals. The mixture is evaporated to 238 degrees if you are using a thermometer, otherwise known as the "soft ball" stage. A small portion of the mass dropped in cold water at that stage can be retrievable as a soft ball. At this time the hot mass is removed from the heat and 12 tablespoons (3/4 cup) of peanut butter is added all at once without stirring. Allow the mixture to cool to lukewarm and add 2 teaspoons of vanilla. On cooling a bit further you should start stirring the mixture to obtain a good blend of all ingredients. Starting the stirring too early means you stir for a long time but starting the stirring late might mean that the candy is formed before it is properly mixed. While you are stirring and you realize the mass is changing color and/or texture it is time to immediately transfer the mass to a slightly buttered platter. This transfer is frequently done best using two people, one to empty the pot and one the spread it around using a buttered spatula. Shortly after the platter has been filled the candy may be cut while it is still warm. Enjoy even scraping the pan.

The second recipe, courtesy of Marion Frey, seems easier and produces excellent results. Blend together 5 cups white sugar, 3 cups brown sugar, 1 cup whole milk and 1 cup evaporated milk. Grease large pan for the product. Heat the mixture and boil for eight minutes and add 10 ounces of peanut butter and ½ pound of butter. Beat with mixer until firm. Transfer to large pan and after cooling a bit the fudge may be cut.

8 - COLLEGE BOUND

Now I think to college he should go
For there is so much to learn and know.

As I recall, Daddy helped me to find a boarding home where I lived for my first year. I had chosen chemistry as my field of study. Since I expressed my need for financial aid I was assigned to the low temperature laboratory of Dr. John Aston. I helped the graduate students doing NYA (National Youth Administration) work at 35 cents an hour. I worked hard to be accepted by these graduate students who were studying the thermodynamic properties of simple molecules. One of my early assignments was the making of thermocouples which were used to measure sensitive temperature changes. I was fortunate to be in that laboratory. As I approached the end of my first year I was offered the opportunity to run the liquid air plant the following year. The plant was in the low temperature lab and the liquid air was used in this and other labs as a trapping agent on vacuum systems. Of course I accepted, but this meant that I would no longer carry a full course load while in college. Now I would be on a divided pay scale, 50 cents/hour from the college and 35 cents/hour from NYA. On the basis of this offer Daddy borrowed the money for me to complete my first year at college. The summer of 1939 marked the last summer that I would spend at home although the following year a two week vacation was extended one week when the college delayed opening for one week because of a polio scare. Other activities included going to the Presbyterian Fellowship on Sundays and I also became involved as a college chapel usher.

My second year at Penn State found me working more and taking fewer courses. I was now living at a different location and I had joined the Nittany Cooperative. At this location was a girls' dormitory with an equal number of men joining them for meals. The operation was a blessing for many students because we all shared in the duties. We had a paid cook and a paid manager. In the springtime I seemed to have some difficulty with some laboratory classes and also with my work. I had removed a metal plug from one of the small compressors to drain a trap. When I replaced the plug I used too much force and cracked the casting which held it. Charlie Brouse, a powerhouse engineer, was called to do the repair and I have him to thank for saving my job. I think Dr. Aston would have fired me on the spot if Charlie had not spoken on my behalf. These events were a low point in my college days but I resolved I would from then on keep an optimistic outlook and in retrospect it worked.

The operation of the liquid air plant at one time grew to be operated around the clock under a contract with the National Defense Research Council. Needless to say I had other people helping me at that time. The college was testing column packings for the distillation of liquid air to obtain oxygen. These studies helped the Air Force to have mobile units for making oxygen for the pilots during the Second World War.

In brief, I used 12 semesters and two summer schools to obtain my BS degree in chemistry. I was originally in the class of 1942 but due to the wartime acceleration of classes my graduation occurred in October of 1943. I must say a few more words about the Nittany Co-op. This group arose out of the necessity of the time and the willingness of the members to devote time to the operation of the organization founded on the principle of shared cooperation. Of course there was an economic advantage for the members. One year my assignment was that of bursar in that I collected the money each month and deposited it to our account. Many romances and marriages grew from these beginnings. I remember well December 7, 1941. While studying and listening to the radio President Roosevelt announced the attack on Pearl Harbor. On that Sunday evening the men gathered early at the Co-op to discuss this tragic event. I estimated that Daddy paid about one-half of my college expenses, around $3000, but I was able to pay this all back and as a matter of fact I was sending some money home while still at college. This was also facilitated by the fact that during my last year at Penn State my pay rate had increased to 75 cents an hour. Early in July I was interviewed in New York for my post college job. I accepted the job while traveling through the Holland tunnel, but there was a hitch, I needed to complete a thesis.

On meeting with Dean Whitmore he flattered me by writing dependability on a tablet and then showing it to the nth power. I completed my laboratory work for my thesis before reporting for work in September. I typed my thesis on a coin-activated typewriter at the 34th street YMCA in New York City.

9 - THE FREY FAMILY

What legacy is wrought
Or what life has taught.

Wayne probed into the past history of the Frey name and then more recently the hobby was one of niece Elaine's favorites. The origin of the name stands for "free." Grandfather did have siblings but to the best of our knowledge no brothers had male children to carry on the name. You have been given most of the story on John Frey already but I will note that he and Lucinda enjoyed about 50 years of marriage.

John and Lucinda's family included 5 sons and one daughter, Clarence, Joseph, Edwin, Susan, Milton and James. Clarence served time in the army in far away places like Alaska and Hawaii but little was seen or heard of him after the death of his mother. He was a Spanish American war veteran. He did marry but had no children and lived his final days in St. Louis. While in the army he did some quilting using some embroidery stitching. Uncle Joe married Aunt Sarah and they had no children. They lived in Johnson City, New York and for years he was a loyal worker associated with the Endicott-Johnson shoe company. Edwin, my father, will be discussed later. Susan married Ike Shoemaker and their children were Camilla, William and Theodore. We children saw much of these cousins for a time. William became a teacher and lived in Illinois. Ted remained in the area. Millie's husband at one time was a farmer with one arm, having lost the arm in an accident. My father was amazed at his one-armed abilities. Uncle Milton became a devoted farm worker for a Mrs. Hess while he was still a teenager. Since her children abandoned her, on her death she left most of her estate to Uncle Milton. The Hess children fought for some inheritance but the case was decided otherwise. He moved near Uncle Joe and he worked for the same shoe company. Uncle Milt gave us the only loving canine pet we ever had, a dog named Ted. One of the things Ted loved was to go coon hunting, which we did on a few occasions.

Uncle Milt was married twice but he had no children. In his declining years Uncle Milt lived with Kenneth and Marion and then finally in the Estella nursing home. Uncle Jim saw active duty in the first World War in France but he never wanted to talk about it. He was a wanderer and I think often he may have been a freight car rider in his travels. He was married two or more times and fathered four or more children but only one son.

Edwin Elmer Ellsworth Frey (1/3/89-5/16/51) was not a complex man. He was a hard working farmer as well as a school teacher. Because of family choices it fell to his lot to care for his parents in their final years. He was a disciplinarian whose most hurtful words sometimes were "go get the razor strap." You see if you needed corporal punishment this strap is what you felt. Mother withheld such treatment but Daddy would use it on his sons. In short, punishment given was usually deserved. He did not seem to be affectionate in the usual sense but when Mother needed something he never seemed to let her down. If Daddy were in the barn and needed a tool from the garage he expected you to run there and back. He planned the fields and gardens to provide for crop rotation and better yields.

Florence Myrtle Decker Frey (3/17/1891-10/12/1947) (m. 2/1/1913) was always present or so it seemed. I think of the many times my laundry box was sent home from college and back again. You see that was the way things were done then. She noted my two separated teeth meant that I would live far from home. She liked to milk the cows and so she would as often as possible. For breakfast she would never be seated until everyone else was content. She loved gardening as I previously indicated and that included flowers. She enjoyed receiving a bunch of hepaticas from the woodland grove in the springtime. You could also bring delight to her eyes by bringing a pail of freshly picked wild berries. She sent us off to school in timely fashion since we would have to walk over a mile. On winter's coldest days she would caution us to stop if necessary at one of the neighbor's houses on the way if we became too cold.

Edwin and Florence had four sons and three daughters. Their eldest, Dorothy Mary (3/28/1914-5/5/1960) married Edward H. MacDonald (b. 2/28/1889) on 5/20/1946. Dorothy was born with a congenital defect that affected an arm and a leg. In time she learned to live with this handicap. Dorothy did a lot of the housework and she loved to wear necklaces of beads which were restrung often. After her death with colitus, her daughter, Florence Marie (12/3/1947-3/9/1999) went to live with Kenneth and Marion. Florence married David A. Minotte (b. 8/1/43) on 10/28/1968 and they had two children.

Kenneth Joseph (1/16/1916-2/20/93) married Marion Hattie Brown 6/14/1935 and they had three sons and three daughters. Their little Carol left us at age five with a rheumatic heart. Dolores, Ronald, Miles, Eugene and Elaine were the other children who are now in retirement or are approaching it. Kenneth's life experiences were many and varied. He was a farmer, county tax assessor, rural mail carrier and grandfather and great grandfather to many offspring. With him all the way was Marion (frequently called Peggy) as they provided a home for Florence after Dorothy's death and later still for Uncle Milt until he went to the Estella nursing home. Kenneth and Marion were able to travel over much of the USA during retirement and even to Australia with Lawrence and Caroline Baumunk. Marion loved quilting and she has made many herself and assisted in making many others.

Lawrence Decker (8/23/1918-7/30/1999) married Leona Genevieve Brown 6/14/1941 and they had two sons and two daughters. Lawrence Decker, Jr., Ina Rose, Donald Lee and Lillian Leona were their children. Larry and Don along with cousins Miles and Eugene were in scouting together and they all went for the top awards of Eagle Scouts and God in Country honors. Here the double cousins doubled up in the interest of youthful growth and development.

Lawrence saw duty in the Pacific theater late in the Second World War. He was a bombardier in the Air Force. He recounts that one of the scariest moments of his active service was weathering a typhoon in a mess hall on Okinawa. He stayed with the reserves on leaving active duty and rose to the rank of Major. After Mother's death Daddy sold the farm to Lawrence who also worked as a rural mail carrier. Both Lawrence and Kenneth were great hunters and they often sent their visitors home with trophies of deer.

Sheldon Ellsworth (b. 4/29/1921) married Uva Steele Gillespie (b. 11/18/1921) on 4/26/1947 in Oak Ridge, TN in the Chapel on the Hill. Our children are John Sheldon and Lisa Louise. More details are found elsewhere in this book.

Alice Marie (2/6/1924-5/23/2004) was married to Firman Harold Eastham (b. 7/20/1914) on 6/29/1947 and they had one daughter, Laura Diana. Alice attended and graduated from Canton High School. She worked for a lady with whom she boarded. After high school she enrolled in the nursing program at the Robert Packer Hospital. She met and married Firman who worked at IBM. Their only child also chose the field of nursing and she met and married a Canadian. Alice was active in church activities right up until being overcome by brain cancer.

Irene Lucinda (8/16/1926-) was married to Robert Leroy Foust (b. 9/29/1920) on 6/14/1947 and for a bit of trivia this was the third of my siblings to choose 6/14 as their wedding day, which was also grandmother Lucinda's birthday. Even though Lucinda was not around to help with the delivery, Irene was born at home. Irene was more of a tomboy than Alice. While three children were born the baby girl, Linda Lee died after only one month. Allen and David, their two sons, are currently employed by the local school system in Montoursville, Pennsylvania. Irene spent much of her later adult life assisting elderly women either by sleeping nearby or by fixing a meal. While she had no nursing training she served her community somewhat as a nurse's aide. At one time she told me she was working 22 hours a day, sleeping nearby and fixing breakfast for one of the three clients. Robert loved antique sales and he made some collection of small items over the years.

Edwin Wayne Allen (3/23/34-9/21/2000) married Deonne Genesta Hartman (b. 3/13/1936) on 3/25/1956 and they had five sons, Edwin Duane, Darryl Eugene, Scott Larue, Douglas Arthur and Jamie M. Wayne was thirteen years younger, so I did not really experience him as a brother at home. By the time I left for college he was four. When Mother died Wayne was thirteen and during the next four years he had many rich experiences with his father. He graduated from Lycoming College and after his marriage to Deonne he went on to become an expert in size reduction operations. He operated a manufacturer's representative business. One son, Darryl, developed the "Three Sisters Farm" north of Pittsburgh, Pennsylvania. The farm features an ecological setting patterned after Indian lore of the companion support of corn, squash and beans. Chickens were added to provide heat and fertilizer. One of the products from this operation was an organically grown salad mix which proved economical. Another son, Scott, is active in the lobbying efforts to save Social Security from those who would change it.

I have only scratched the surface of my siblings' lives, loves and professions. I will not attempt to pursue the vivid life and activities of the many nieces and nephews because I cannot do justice to their successes or failures in some cases, but perhaps one of them can take on that assignment. Suffice it to say many are now grandparents and would have much to offer to the history of the extended Frey family.

Here is some background
That we have found.

Harrison Ridge (1/28/1829-7/17/1901) was born in Liberty Township, Tioga County, Pennsylvania and was the son of John and Mary (Dawson) Ridge. Mary Kimble (2/14/1830-7/2/1871) was born in Fairfield Township, Lycoming County, Pennsylvania and was the daughter of Henry and Sophia (Slout) Kimble. She married Harrison on 1/19/1851 in Jackson Township, Lycoming County, Pennsylvania. Together they had eleven children and the eighth child was Mary Emma (5/25/1866-8/16/1939). Harrison enlisted as a private in Company I, 207th PA, V.I., 3 Brig., 3 Div. 9th A.C. He served at Point of Rocks, Virginia and at Ft. Steedman and at Petersburg, Virginia. He was severely wounded and for a time had pneumonia. He was honorably discharged in June 1865.

Mary Emma Ridge married Henry Decker (d. 10/29/1927) April 1886 and they had seven daughters and one son. Mother was the third daughter. Aunt Lulu was married with one daughter, Mildred. Aunt Lily was married to Uncle Jack and they had no children. Aunt Frances was married twice but there were no children. These three sisters lived in Philadelphia. Aunt Mae married Elmer Miller and they lived on a farm near East Point. They had a family of twelve children and nearby lived Aunt Betty who married Carl Schanbacher and they had two children. Aunt Aldora married Uncle Howard and they lived in Riverdale, Maryland with their two sons. Uncle Miles was married twice, first to Aunt Irene and then to Aunt Polly, but he had no children. Uncle Miles operated a garage in Williamsport, Pennsylvania but he had a lifetime hobby of fishing. We always compared Lawrence with him since they were both tall and loved to fish.

Since the preceding gives an account of Mother's ancestors I will now turn to the Battins which was my

paternal Mother's ancestral connection. John Battin married
Elizabeth in Berkshire, England and is next found in
Pennsylvania. In 1714 he purchased 150 acres in Chester
County. One of their many children was John, who was
listed in E. Caln as a freeman in 1740 (probable birth 1719).
He was listed as a carpenter. John was received as a member
of Friends on 11/21/1741 and on 4/3/1742 he married
Mary Marshall (b. 1720) daughter of William Marshall at
West Bradford. Mary Marshall's grandfather, John
Marshall, came from Elton, Darbyshire, England in 1687
and settled in Blickley Township, Philadelphia,
Pennsylvania. In 1688 he married Sarah Smith who came
from Leicester, England. Mary Marshall's father, William
(2/11/1692-1727) married Mary Sellers (b. 10/13/1687)
who was the daughter of Samuel Sellers (1655-1732).
Samuel emigrated with the vessels that came with William
Penn in 1682 and in 1684 he married Anne Gibbons in
Darby.

One of John and Mary Battin's children was John Battin (10/20/1749-10/24/1835) who was married in 1766 to a native of Ireland, Susanna McDermitt (5/9/1749-12/12/1826). John was in the Revolutionary War. The battle of Brandywine 9/11/1777 was very near his home. He is listed in Harrisburg as Batten, John Jun., Pvt., 1st Battalion, 8th Co., W. Bradford Township, 7th Class, Capt. Jacob Buffington in charge, Class Return for period 1777-80. During 1793-1794 he appears in Muncy based on land acquisitions. In 1811 he moved from Muncy to Shunk with some of his children. One of John and Susanna's children was Marshall (12/23/1784-12/4/1875) who married Mary Hogeland (12/30/1788-12/2/1880) on 3/27/1809. Marshall was a blacksmith and an Elder in the Quaker Church. Tradition has it that Marshall and Mary walked 30 miles to Eldredsville to be married by Squire Eldred. Marshall owned a large tract of land on which he raised many cattle and horses. His farm was a station for the Underground Railroad which assisted slaves who were trying to reach Canada. At night his sons would go to other farms that were hiding slaves and then guide them over Indian trails to Marshall's farm. When it was thought safe they then would be moved on toward their destination. The routing of the railroad was from Lincoln Falls via Wheelerville to Canton and northward to New York State. It is not known whether quilts or any other signaling device were used in the operation. Of course, I might point out that his granddaughter Lucinda made many quilts but I feel that this had no connection to previous events.

Joseph Battin (5/6/1812-5/12/1890) was one of Marshall and Mary's sons who married Nancy Bagley (d. 2/1/1876) on 12/5/1836 in Canton by Justice Asa Pratt. Joseph was a farmer in Fox Township and Lucinda was one of Joseph and Mary's children who later married John Frey. Marshall and Mary were both buried at Elklands (now an historical site). Elklands is located just outside of Fox Township in Elkland Township. Fox Township prior to 1839 was a part of Elkland Township.

11 - On the Job

Now to work you should go
For by your efforts you may grow.

September 1943 found me at the YMCA on 34th Street in Manhattan and riding the nickel subway to the Nash Building at 134th Street for work. The work was scheduled for six days and eight hours per day. Saturday was an overtime day so my initial pay was 52 dollars/week. I was working for the Kellex Corporation, an offshoot of M. W. Kellogg Corp. of engineering fame. We were on a secret mission which picked up the name Manhattan Project. The project culminated in the design, construction and operation of the first uranium hexafluoride gaseous diffusion plant at Oak Ridge, Tennessee known at the K-25 plant. This plant was nearly a mile long but it was folded in the middle so that it was U-shaped with the control room centrally located. This long structure had many units with a typical one having six vessels containing packing through which the process gas would travel in going from unit to unit. The design was like a huge distillation column so that in operation a concentrated uranium 235 gas would be the product. The units contained a stainless steel valve. It was determined early on that it took an experienced welder to produce a good seam on this valve. You see the task lying ahead of us was to vacuum test the construction piping and connections so that no inleakage of nitrogen would occur since the system operated at sub-atmospheric pressure. This is a very brief description of the job which is to come.

As noted above I completed my thesis and attended graduation in October 1943 and after two months at the YMCA I moved to an apartment on Riverside Drive near 116th Street with a friend from the Nittany Co-op. His assignment was also war-related, since it involved the Norden bomb sight. I still returned to the YMCA on Sunday mornings to join fellow worshippers who usually traveled to the Marble Collegiate Church to hear Norman Vincent

Peale preach. A few times the group attended the Riverside Presbyterian Church where Harry Emerson Fosdick was the pastor. Work was six days a week, but some time was found to attend shows at Radio City Music Hall with the Rockettes. I was in the New Years Eve crowd on Broadway for the 1944 New Year. I recollect that after this celebration I bought a US Savings Bond to attend a movie.

Early in 1944 I was traveling to Jersey City to participate in testing a trial setup. The apparatus being tested was connected to the vacuum pump with a side connection for the leak detector. By probing the apparatus with a tiny stream of helium the leak detector would give a wild gauge indication if a leak were probed. It was possible to detect small leaks and when successful repairs were made the apparatus could be given a prolonged test to see if loss of vacuum occurred. These operations would be repeated over and over again in the near future. On traveling home one time I fell asleep and went right by my subway stop so I had to turn around to get home.

Early in April 1944 I caught a train for Knoxville, Tennessee. At that time one could leave New York for New Orleans every 8 hours. On arrival in Knoxville, I was met by my new boss, Dr. Armistead. He delivered me to an Army-style dormitory in West Village, Oak Ridge, Tennessee where I lived for the next few months. Oak Ridge was behind a security fence and remained so until after the second World War was over. While this was a "secret city," Oak Ridge became the fifth largest city in Tennessee exceeded by only Nashville, Memphis, Chattanooga and Knoxville. The electrical demands for the Oak Ridge area were to be supplied by the TVA hydroelectric plants. The travel to work usually involved a closed trailer at first with one security stop. The K-25 area was a beehive of activity because of all the new construction.

Soon Dr. Armistead's group grew by leaps and bounds with new arrivals being largely engineering students from General Electric and other companies. This core group of about thirty men served as a basis for the vacuum testing division which at one time included about 900 men and women. The supervisors who were assigned often had to report 2-3 hours early in order to properly line up the work for the next shift. During the latter part of 1944 the shifts were 6 AM – 6 PM and from 6 PM - 6 AM, seven days a week. At the end of 1944 it was now accepted that vacuum testing was an operating function and the group was taken over by Carbide and Chemicals Corp.

The plant had control stations in building units to monitor the operation and if an inleakage of nitrogen was detected the unit might need to be by-passed. The control room also had similar information. Some time was spent following these stations. Daily some product was removed at the final station for transfer to another location for further processing. The year 1945 soon demonstrated the end result of our efforts with the dropping of two atomic bombs on Japanese cities. The war in the Far East was suddenly brought to an end.

By now I felt that I wanted to return to activities more closely related to chemistry than the operational or engineering activity which I was doing. I was earning about $300/mo. when I joined Dr. Lafferty's group in the research laboratory. Among the projects I worked on was one testing chlorotrifluoroethylene polymer which was used in certain plant applications. A publication resulted from this work and I remember another case of helping an engineering MIT (I believe) student do a special project which had to be completed in six weeks. Now having more time I looked for extension courses taught by the University of Tennessee at Oak Ridge as a way of continuing my graduate studies. I was once asked why I wanted to join the "know it all" group which we knew who had their PhD degrees. My reply was that I did not think this cocky attitude was necessarily a part of the degree. I can attest that a few years later when I received my PhD it was quite obvious that there was much more to learn. The next significant event in my life was that I was about to meet my life's partner, my wife. The account of her early life, schooling and activities will follow the presentation of some family photographs.

These pictures first present the Frey family and then the Gillespies. Within the two families, the pictures first depict ancestors and then Sheldon's and Uva's generation. Every attempt has been made to include pictures of all nieces and nephews.

Figure 1: Lucinda Battin Frey 1857-1925

Figure 2: John Frey 1854-1932

Figure 3: Mary Emma Ridge Decker 1866-1939

Figure 4: Henry Decker d. 1927

Figure 5: Florence Decker Frey

Figure 6: Edwin Elmer Ellsworth Frey & Family, 1927

Left back to right:
Edwin holding Irene, Florence
Kenneth, Dorothy, Lawrence, Sheldon, & Alice

Figure 7: South Street School

The one room school house where Sheldon attended school through the eighth grade. The building has seen better days. It is now used as a hunting cabin.

Figure 8: Shunk High School

The front and left side housed the Shunk grade school while the right and back side housed the Shunk High School.

Figure 9: Dorothy Frey & Edward H. McDonald's Wedding Day

Figure 10: Marion Brown & Kenneth Frey's Wedding Day

Left to Right: Florence & Edwin Frey, Marion & Kenneth Frey, Anna & Lewis Brown

Figure 11: Leona Brown & Lawrence Decker Frey

Figure 12: Uva Gillespie & Sheldon Frey's Wedding Day

Figure 13: Alice Frey & Firman Eastham

Figure 14: Irene Frey and Bob Foust

Figure 15: Frey Brothers & Sisters, 1989

Back Standing: Alice Frey Eastham, Uva, Kenneth, Irene & Bob Foust; Middle Sitting: Firman Eastham, Sheldon, Marion; Front Sitting: Deonne & Wayne

Figure 16: Lisa & John Fisher's Wedding, 1990

Back left to front right: Lawrence, Alice, Dean & Dolores Frey Hartford, Peggy & Kenneth, Wayne & Deonne, Scott, Leona, Uva (mother of the bride), Kim (Scott's wife), & Sheldon (father of the bride)

Figure 17: Florence Marie McDonald Minotte

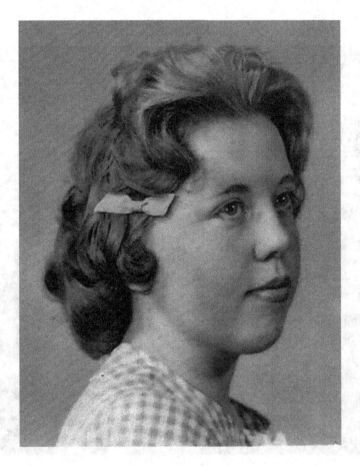

Florence , daughter of Dorothy and Edward McDonald.

Figure 18: Kenneth & Marion Frey's Children

Back left to front right: Ronald, Miles, Gene, Dolores & Elaine

Figure 19: Lawrence & Leona Frey & Children

Christmas 1995: Back left to front right: Lawrence, Leona, Lillian, Don, Ina & Larry

Figure 20: Sheldon Frey – Penn State University, 1940

Figure 21: Uva & Sheldon Frey with Fishers

1998 Frey Family Reunion in Shunk at the cabin. The kids first visit to Shunk! Left to right: Lisa Frey Fisher, Sheldon & Uva Frey, John, Arman James Sheldon & Aigulia Uva Louise Fisher

Figure 22: John Sheldon Frey with Gillespie Cousins

New River, West Virginia Raft Trip 1995
Back left to right: Michael Bell, Christopher Bell, John
Fisher, Lisa Frey Fisher, John Frey, Donna Bell

Figure 23: 1990 John Fisher & parents

Mary, John Roy & James Fisher

Figure 24: Sheldon's ISI co-workers & friends

Pat & Fred Rosso and Shelly & Abu Rahman

Figure 25: Frey/Fisher Fun, 2003

Left back to right front: John Fisher, Uva & Sheldon Frey, Arman James Sheldon, Aigulia Uva Louise & Lisa Frey Fisher

Taken shortly after we all moved into our new home in 2003. Featured in a Winchester Star article on adoptive families.

Figure 26: Alice, Firman & Laura Eastham

Figure 27: Irene Foust & Children

Figure 28: Alan & his wife, Pam Foust

Alan, David & Irene Foust

Figure 29: Wayne & Deonne Frey's Sons, 2004

Left to right: Jamie, Duane, Doug, Darrell & Scott

Figure 30: Reunion Picnic Fun

Figure 31: More Reunion Picnic Fun

Figure 32: Cora Lee & William Steele Family

Back left to front right:: Uva Vesta Steele Gillespie, William Steele, Cora Lee Steele, and Rex Steele

Figure 33: Cora Lee Steele - "Dranny"

Figure 34: Making Music, 1947
*

Uva Steele & John Blair Gillespie

Figure 35: Uva Steele & John Blair Gillespie

Figure 36: Three Gillespie sisters with their Mother

Mary Jane, Uva Steele (mother), Uva Steele (daughter)
better known as Johnnie & Catherine Lee

Figure 37: Tazewell County Club at Radford

Tazewell County Club at Radford College

Back Row—Elizabeth Ann Dorton, Kathleen Hill, Bluefield, Virginia; Mary Nancy Claytor, Ruby Harris, Thompson Valley, Virginia; Seated, middle row: Anna Lee Neel, Cove Creek, Virginia; Nell Harman, Maxwell, Va.; Eunice Rhudy, Thompson Valley, Va.; Frances Thompson, Thompson Valley, Va.; Bettie Flo Brooks, Richlands, Va.; Kathleen Leffel, Shawver Mill. Front row: Johnnie Gillespie, Cedar Bluff, Va.; Mildred Rhudy, Thompson Valley; Margaret Louise Bowen, Tazewell, Va.; Vivian Allen, Richlands, Va.; Mary Jane Gillespie, Cedar Bluff, Va.

Figure 38: Sisters Preparing for German Dance Club Ball

Mary Jane and Johnnie Gillespie were two of the founders of the German Dance Club.

Figure 39: The Sisters Three on Easter Sunday

Catherine, Mary Jane and Johnnie Gillespie

Figure 40: Three Gillespie Sisters visiting Salvo, NC, 1999

Uva Frey, Catherine Warner, Mary Jane Gordanier

Figure 41: Catherine & Scott Warner, 1947

Sheldon & Johnnie's wedding day, 4/26/47. Catherine is looking forward to the birth of her first of three daughters, Mary Catherine

Figure 42: Mary Jane Gillespie

Figure 43: Johnnie Gillespie

Figure 44: The Apple of His Eye

Figure 45: Headline should read S.E. Frey

PAGE FOUR

Miss Gillespie Becomes Bride of E. S. Frey

Miss Uva Steele Gillespie and Sheldon Elsworth Frey were united in marriage in a ceremony performed Saturday morning in the Chapel-on-the-Hill at Oak Ridge, Tenn., by the Rev. Robert Lee Thomas.

The bride is the daughter of Mr. and Mrs. John Blair Gillespie of Cedar Bluff and the groom is the son of Mr. and Mrs. Edwin E. Frey of Wheelerville, Pa.

Decorations of the Chapel were ferns, dogwood blossoms, white phlox and candelabra. Mrs Caroline Disfrow sang, "I Love Thee", and "At Dawning." A program of organ music was played by Mrs. Robert Siebert.

Given in marriage by her father, the bride wore a dress of biege crepe and a matching hat of lace. She carried a white orchid bouqet.

Her attendants were Miss Evelyn Harris and Miss Mary Rose Bannister, of Oak Ridge. They wore costumes of aqua and pink and carried bouquets of snapdragoons.

Bill McColy served the groom as best man. Ushers were Robert Rainy and Forrest Willis.

The couple left by airplane for a trip to Miami Beach, Fla. Mr. and Mrs. Frey will reside in Oak Ridge Tenn.

The bride attended V P I. and Radford College. She is now employed in the laboratory of Carbon and Carbide Co. The groom was a graduate of Pennsylvania State College and is at present a research chemist in the Chemical Research Laboratory at Oak Ridge.

Figure 46: Christmas Greetings 1947!

Figure 47: The Gillespies circa 1963

Back left to front: right: Catherine & Scott Warner, Sheldon Frey, Don Gordanier, Uva & Susan Warner, Johnnie Frey, Mary Jane Gordanier, Mary Catherine Warner, John & Uva Gillespie, John Sheldon Frey, Victoria Louise Gordanier, Lisa Louise Frey

Figure 48: Gillespie Reunion, 1995

Back row: Vicki Gordanier, Michael & Donna Bell, Susan & Dean Daniels, Uva & John Stanley, John Frey, Lisa & John Fisher; Middle row: Allie, Drew & Mark Murfin, Joseph & Will Stanley; Front row: Christopher Bell, Don & Mary Jane Gordanier, Catherine Warner, Uva & Sheldon Frey

Figure 49: The Three Sisters & Their Daughters, 1999

On Vacation in Salvo, NC:
From left to right: Lisa Frey Fisher, Uva Warner Stanley,
Susan Warner Daniels, Uva Frey, Catherine Warner, Mary
Catherine Warner, Mary Jane Gordanier, Vicki Gordanier,
Donna Gordanier Bell

Figure 50: Picnicking with Catherine, 2001

Standing: Mary Jane & Donald Gordanier, Uva & Sheldon
Frey; Seated: Catherine Warner & John Frey

Figure 51: Sheldon & Uva's 70th Birthday Party

Figure 52: More 70th Birthday Fun

Pete Petroff, Sheldon Frey, Lisa Fisher, Bobby Petroff

Figure 53: Kitty Simon's Thanksgiving Wish

13 - The Gillespie Family

Was life kind or rough

From Pounding Mill to Cedar Bluff.

I, Uva Steele Gillespie, was born 11/18/1921, the third daughter of Uva Vesta Steele and John Blair Gillespie. Even as a baby I was nicknamed Johnnie since a boy was hoped for and didn't arrive. This later had some interesting results; for example, in college I received notice to report for ROTC. My older sisters and I were all born in Pounding Mill but grew up in Cedar Bluff which we knew as home.

Catherine Lee, my oldest sister, was born in 1916 and Mary Jane on 7/3/20, a mere 16 months earlier than I. Mary Jane and I were close friends then and throughout life. Grandfather, William Steele, gave me a lamb that was a joy for a time, but it overate and though life saving efforts were tried, it died. Once I recall an April Fool's party when the hostess served an apricot on cake which looked like toast and I declined partaking by saying I did not like an egg on toast.

My Mother, Uva Vesta, like her Mother before her was a lover of flowers. She loved to cook and crochet. She attended Martha Washington in Abington where she did some painting of china. She attended Lynchburg College and she liked to play the piano. It was a treat for all to hear a duet by her and Poppa John on his "fiddle" of an old time waltz or some other favorite number. Needless to say these musical interludes would often require much coaxing to have them occur. After Sheldon entered her life as a son-in-law she would frequently refer to him as a damn Yankee.

Uva Vesta Steele (9/27/88-9/18/1976) had a younger brother Rex who became a veterinarian. John Blair Gillespie (8/28/1887-8/31/1971) was born at Witten Mills. John had six brothers and five sisters. John attended Lynchburg College and became a traveling salesman for the S. B. Hite and Co. In his later years he was the postmaster at Cedar Bluff for 8 years. As a young man John loved baseball and he liked to go out with other men to hear the hounds howl as they sought their prey. His father was John Floyd Gillespie (Grandpa Foxy) and his mother was Mary Catherine Graham. At the time of my father's death only one of his siblings survived. Aunt Bess had married John Wilson, an Episcopal minister, and they spent several years in China as missionaries.

My maternal grandmother, Cora Lee was a Claypoole and a McGuire. She married William Steele who was a very successful farmer. We children called her Dranny because she wasn't interested in being called Granny. Dranny's life is legendary among her descendants. As a young married woman, she traveled cross country by train to Mexico to attend bullfights. Many of us wonder if this is where she heard the name "Uva" which means grape in Spanish.

Catherine wrote some memories of Dranny and she recalled her travels. When she went on a trip like one to Anderson, Indiana where she attended a Christian meeting

she would pack sandwiches of ground ham and eggs.
Another trip took her to the San Francisco Exposition in the
early 1900's.

Their cellar was filled with fruits and vegetables.
Apples came in by the wagon loads from two orchards.
Black walnuts were also stored in the cellar because Pa
Steele loved to crack them to eat with his sips of whiskey
which he hid in the basement.

When Uva and John eloped to be married at Aunt
Oakley's, Dranny followed on the next train. She grew to
like John and would often tell her daughter, "Uva if you
looked the world over you would never have found a man
who would make a better husband than John." She won
many medals when she was in school. She had a flower
room above the kitchen which was heated in winter by a
ceiling register above the kitchen stove. Potted plants
included geraniums, begonias, Christmas cactus and
impatiens. She was ardent in her Christian faith and she read
the Bible through many times.

Mary Jane adds some additional recollections. A book agent leaving the train at Pounding Mill would find his way to her door. Mary Jane loved to peruse her library. Dranny taught me water conservation because she noted that water from the spigot should be put to use. After Pa Steele died Dranny would alternate living with her son, Rex, or with Uva. During these occasions Mary Jane elected to sleep with Dranny since Catherine and Johnnie did not wish to sleep with her. She taught school between Pounding Mill and Claypool Hill. She rode a horse with Rex in front and Uva behind. On one occasion someone spooked the horse with a loud noise, Uva fell off and carried a lifetime scar on her face.

Now Johnnie loved Dranny's flower room. Dranny enjoyed nice things. She always had a maid and a cook while her husband lived. He died during the great depression and was buried on the farm. She was always curious about any fellow who came calling. She had served 56 years as a country correspondent to Clinch Valley News since she was

16 years old. She performed a similar task for the Bluefield Daily Telegraph after its establishment 50 years earlier, 1889. In an article that appeared in 1939, she recalled her own wedding to W. B. Steele on 3/24/1887. The wedding was at 1 PM and the crowd of wedding guests spent the remainder of the day "until after dark" consuming the wedding feast of "thirty chickens and all the trimmings". Her news gathering was familiar to all with the question, "have you been anywhere, killed anybody or stole anything?" She often chose to report how many times she had completed reading the bible. She did so by referring to herself in the third person. At age 72 she was still active in her news gathering activity.

From Northern Ireland to Tazewell
What a story they can tell.

I t is my belief that Margaret Graham was a moving
force in the migration of the Grahams from the
County of Down, Ireland to America in 1770.
Margaret knew Joseph Johnston who was born near Dublin
in 1745 and who emigrated in 1768. The reports from
Joseph were no doubt favorable so the Graham party grew.
Robert was 20 years old and recently married to Mary Craig
and a brother made up the party. Samuel Graham was born
on the voyage of Robert and Mary from Ireland to America
in 1770. From Philadelphia they went to North Carolina
and shortly thereafter Margaret married Joseph Johnston.
They moved to the nearby York district of South Carolina
and some of their descendants were prominent citizens of
Cleveland, TN. Samuel married Rachel Montgomery who
was the daughter of Col. John Montgomery (from Scotland)

who served in the Revolutionary War with George Rodgers Clark in the Illinois Campaign against the British. Samuel served as volunteer Captain in the war of 1812 and was promoted to Major during services at Norfolk, Virginia. He also served in the Virginia legislature for two years.

Samuel and Rachel had thirteen children and the next to the youngest was William Leander born in 1820. William Leander Graham was a natural born soldier, whose father and grandfather had served their country before him. When the war between the states broke out he was made Lieutenant Colonel of the 16th Regiment of Calvary Volunteers in the Confederate Army. He served in campaigns in the valley of Virginia, Pennsylvania and Maryland. Late in 1864, he was captured near Moorefield, Hardy County, West Virginia and was sent to the prison camp at Camp Chase, Ohio for the remainder of the war. His unit repulsed the Federal troops at Saltville and also helped to save Lynchburg. His regiment and that of the 22nd Virginia Cavalry attacked the forces of Gen. Hunter near

Salem and inflicted heavy losses on the enemy and captured artillery pieces and destroyed ordinance. After the war he was a circuit court judge for Buchanan and Wise Counties. During President Cleveland's first administration he was US Marshall for the Western District of Virginia.

He married Louisa Bowen Thompson, daughter of Archibald Thompson, Esq. who lived and died in Thompson Valley. One of their six children was Mary Catherine Graham who became the wife of John Floyd Gillespie (Grandpa Foxy) as noted above. Archibald was the son of Louisa Bowen and John who was the son of William Thompson (1722-1788). Louisa Bowen was the daughter of Rees Bowen who was killed in 1780 at King's Mountain, South Carolina. Rees Bowen was the grandson of Moses and Rebecca Bowen who came from Wales in 1698. The Bowens first settled in Massachusetts, then Pennsylvania, Delaware, Maryland and finally Virginia. Their son John, who was the father of Rees, was born about 1750 and Rees married Levisa Smith (1750-1834) in 1768. A daughter Margaret was to become the wife of Tom Gillespie.

Lieutenant Rees Bowen and Levisa Smith were married in 1768 and settled at Maiden Springs, Tazewell County and were reported to be the second white family to settle in Tazewell County. They built a stockade around their house (1772-3) for protection from the Indians. About 1776 news reached them that the Indians from Ohio were on the warpath, murdering and scalping victims as they traveled. The men went out to intercept them but the Indians slipped by the men. With no man left to protect the women and children, diminutive Levisa took charge. When rounding up the cows for milking she observed a fresh moccasin print in the area. She dressed in her son's clothes and ordered an African American woman to wear her husband's clothes. Levisa liked to wear a man's hat and though there were other women in the stockade the African American was the only one over whom she had authority. Levisa carried a rifle and the African American carried a stick resembling a rifle. They marched around the stockade that night and any time the African American resisted Levisa threatened to shoot her. The next day the men returned and later the Indian campfire was found nearby. Levisa and her companion had saved the stockade from attack.

King's Mountain, South Carolina became the site of a major battle of the Revolutionary War in the South (1780). Major Ferguson was attempting to move North to advance the British cause. Colonels Shelby and Sevier and their group of "over mountain" men arrived to resist this attempt. Major Ferguson was killed and the British forces were severely defeated in the battle. It served to delay Cornwallis moving to the North and it proved to be a turning point of the war in the South. Lieutenant Rees Bowen lost his life at King's Mountain but as noted in this chapter two of his daughters married into the Gillespie family.

In Highland Scots, Gillespie means "Attendant to the Bishop." A number of the early Scottish Gillespies were Presbyterian ministers. The Gillespies encountered in this book came from Northern Ireland. Tom Gillespie (d. 1789) and wife Eleanor had ten children. Thomas Gillespie was the second child of the union and in 1742 he was settled on the Cowpasture River near the head of the James River. He served on a Rowan County jury in 1764. Thomas Gillespie (d. 1842) married Margaret Bowen (d. 1799) in 1781. William Gillespie was the second son of six children. Tom was Col. under Col. Sevier and in the Point Pleasant Battle in 1774 he was one of three men credited for turning the tide of battle. He also was in the King's Mountain battle.

William Gillespie (1784-1875) married Nancy Harrison (1795-1822) in 1810. Thomas H. was the second of nine children born of this union. Nancy's father from Birmingham, England was in the Revolutionary War. William (1806) was Captain 2nd Batt., 112 Regt., and he went to Norfolk in 1812. In 1819 he was Lieut. Colonel 112

Regt., 17 Brig. 3 Division of Militia. In 1821 he served in the House of the Delegates. Thomas H. Gillespie (1812-1894) married Mary Ann Rader (1818-1890) in 1833. John Floyd was the seventh of eleven children of this union. Thomas served in many public offices. He was commissioner of revenue for the western district in 1835, deputy sheriff 1840-5 and House of Delegates 1846-8. He was a potent force for Christian causes through the auspices of the Christian (Disciples) Church. His high standards gave strength and inspiration to the Christian cause in this area. John Floyd (Grandpa Foxy) has already been cited above.

15 - SISTERS THREE

There were Gillespie sisters three
Catherine, Mary Jane and Johnnie.

Catherine was the oldest sister born in 1916 and after college she taught school for several years. She married Scott Warner of Cedar Bluff after he returned from several years in a Japanese prison camp near Manila. For several years he owned and operated a frozen food locker plant in Cedar Bluff. Both he and Catherine were very active members in the Cedar Bluff Presbyterian Church. Their children included Mary Catherine, named after a great grandmother, Susan and Uva. Mary became a feature writer for newspapers and married Steven MacDonald who is now President of Lebanon Valley State College. They have one son named John. Susan was married to Henry Wilson and raised two children, Charles and Amy. She now lives near Richmond, Virginia with her husband Dean Daniels. Uva taught school after college and

lives in Orange, Virginia with her husband John Stanley.
They have two sons, Joseph and William.

Mary Jane attended Radford College. She and
Johnnie were two of the founders of the German Dance
Club. First she majored in home economics and graduated
from Radford College. She served as a dietitian at the Clinch
Valley Clinic until the staff kept disappearing to the draft.
She then went to the Hercules Powder Plant at Radford to
work as a laboratory technician along side her sister,
Johnnie. She fell in love with a tall, handsome
Midwesterner, her supervisor by the name of Donald
Gordanier. They were married when the Radford plant
closed and moved to Wilmington where their first daughter,
Donna Jane, was born. After a year or two in Kalamazoo,
Michigan, they moved to Oak Ridge where Johnnie and her
husband were working. While they lived in Oak Ridge,
Victoria Louise, a second daughter was born. Later Donald
Gordanier was transferred to Paducah, Kentucky where
another gaseous diffusion UF6 plant was built. Mary Jane

took further training in elementary education and later also in library sciences. She was in the Paducah Public School System for 24 years both in elementary as well as high school teaching. In 1975 her library at Paducah Tilghman High School was chosen as the most improved and most outstanding in the state of Kentucky. The Kentucky Education TV televised action in the library for a day. One of Mary Jane's hobbies was to make clay beads. Pairs of beads were selected for two local craft shows at the Art Gallery. Donna Jane married Michael Bell who served one year in Viet Nam. They have one son, Christopher, who is now raising a family. Meanwhile Donna and Mike are Minnesotans who have a real estate and beef cattle interest in Burkes Garden, Tazewell County, Virginia. Victoria married Mark Murfin and their children Allie and Drew are either finishing college or courting potential spouses. Donald and Mary Jane died on Easter Sunday in 2004 a few minutes apart and in different places, a poignant day.

Johnnie, as I was called, had besides the lamb a dog named Nipper who I liked to make over. Sometimes I would try to put some of my clothes on him. I learned to swim in the dam waters that supplied the Goodwin Woolen Mill which initially ran by water power in the Clinch River below our home. The Goodwin patterns were very popular. Later when electricity became more readily available this plant closed and the operation was moved to North Carolina near Boone. My first year of college was at Virginia Polytechnic Institute (VPI) and for one year Mary Jane left Radford College to be with me. The threat of geometry drove both of us to Radford for the next year. After two years of college I went to the University of Virginia to become a nurse. This did not last long because I realized that this was not my calling.

I went home to teach school at Steelesburg. I also taught underprivileged girls in some home-making skills through an NYA (National Youth Administration) program. As the Radford Plant became active I went there as a laboratory technician in the powder plant. In 1945, as the war was ending, the powder plant closed and I went to the K-25 plant at Oak Ridge, Tennessee as a laboratory technician in Industrial Hygiene.

16 - THE CHEMIST MEETS THE TECHNICIAN

Now a dancing we did go
For a long life – How were we to know?

In our secured city we were not typical Tennesseeans. We came from all over and settled there along the Clinch River which flows by Oak Ridge. Amid this background was Roger Knox from Berkeley, California whose hobby was collecting folk dances and recordings appropriate to the dance. He started a group of interested dancers who enjoyed doing various European dances such as waltzes, hambo, little man in a fix, polkas, tarantello, and many others including the ever popular traditional American square dance and the Virginia reel. His classes were held weekly in a school gymnasium. I had been attending for a short time when one night as frequently occurred some new faces appeared. I did not ask a certain young lady to be my partner for a square dance because I could not see her dancing in high heels. Nevertheless

Johnnie captured me from the beginning as the following lines bear witness. In June of 1946 a group of us spent a weekend in the Smokies and on returning I composed the following to "my gypsy" after a popular song at that time.

There within a sheltered nook,

Close beside a mountain brook,

In the forest deep and shady,

I longed for my gypsy lady.

My gypsy lady tanned and brown,

And for me – Toast of the Town.

Silently she walked on and then

I stopped to admire her again.

By the rippling woodland stream

She paused to rest and to dream.

And dream she did of things worthwhile

As I could see from her smile.

The trail wound up the hillside steep

The slowly footsteps seemed to creep.

Perhaps those legs and feet were tired

On the lady which I admired.

There were flowers pink and white

Sheer cliffs too were quite a sight.

As ruler for this woodland realm

My gypsy lady takes the helm.

Recall one moment if I dared

For when she said for me she cared

My heart skipped a beat and then

I longed for my gypsy again.

As the moon soared over the hill,

Then it was a pleasant thrill

Just to hold my gypsy tight

And to kiss her a sweet goodnight.

At K-25 we worked in the same building and while I was in research she served as a technician in a works or production group. We lived in separate dormitory units but we could travel to work together and eat at cafeterias and I often treated her to such, especially after dancing classes. We enjoyed many movies together and from our dormitories we could walk to the theater. We also made a few group trips to the Smoky Mountains and to a lodge facility near Fontana Dam. These trips were always brief though the one to Fontana included dancing.

On one occasion when leaving the dancing class Johnnie was not feeling well and on reporting to the hospital she needed and received an emergency appendectomy. I stood by and was able to let her family know that all was well. On her 25th birthday, I gave her a gardenia corsage which she wore in her hair and we ate at the Guest House. We visited in her home at Cedar Bluff one wintry weekend in January. Our trip to my home was a bit more involved since we arrived just ahead of a snowstorm. Johnnie had received a shot of penicillin in beeswax a few days prior to our trip. Our arrival called for a doctor's visit since she had an allergic reaction to either the penicillin or the beeswax. The doctor arrived in the early night hours close behind the snowplow and he left me in charge of a hypodermic needle and a supply of adrenalin. I gave the patient shots until the crises had passed. Subsequently we found more than half of the patients receiving this lot of penicillin had similar reactions to it.

Included in this paragraph are some excerpts from my letter to Johnnie's parents asking for her hand in marriage. " --- For the occasion would be to ask consent of Johnnie's parents to take her from them by marriage. But this kind of taking is more one of giving. I want Johnnie to have all those things which are so necessary for her happiness. For me to promise to be good to her, clothe her, shelter her, feed her etc. seems somewhat inadequate for she richly deserves all my heart and hands can afford. It is unfortunate that I am in Oak Ridge with you in Cedar Bluff because I would like to see a toast being offered and a joyful tear being shed to celebrate the occasion. My sentimentality comes from my dad who struggled to keep back a tear as Johnnie and I were leaving my home. Believe me, Johnnie looks fine and feels fine, in fact she has been positively radiant since she rested following her trip to Pennsylvania. --- Knowing that you both are very fine people and wishing you would call me son, I will be happy to be son-in-law. Sincerely with love, Shelly."

We were married on Saturday April 26, 1947 with the bride's parents, her sister Catherine, and brother-in-law Scott Warner in attendance. We were one of many couples married in the army-style "Chapel-on-Hill" during those early Oak Ridge days. On the way to the Knoxville airport we enjoyed the mimosa trees in bloom. Our DC-3 flight to Miami made one stop in Atlanta on the way. The honeymooners at Miami Beach enjoyed the visit and Johnnie, a great sun worshiper, obtained a good suntan during that week.

Now as a married couple we obtained a one-bedroom apartment in a unit containing two one-bedroom apartments and two two-bedroom apartments. Shortly after our marriage we desired to have a dog. We made arrangements to obtain a pedigree dachshund, Hertzel, from the owner in Alabama. One day we received a phone call from the airport saying that the dog was there. We rode buses to the airport and planned to bring him home the same way. You know, we ended up paying a taxi $9.00 for the trip home. Later after Hertzel was sire for a litter we chose a puppy called Johann which we gave to Scott and Catherine.

Shortly after Donna Jane's birth, Johnnie and Catherine made a trip to Delaware to pay their respects and their trip included a side visit to New York to do some shopping. I met Johnnie in Knoxville on her return trip. She had bought a Handmacher suit and an inexpensive fur coat. This was early fall of 1946 and I was kidded later about marrying her for her fur coat. Don, Mary Jane and Donna Jane next moved to Kalamazoo, MI where Don's father owned a hardware store. Don was looking for an opportunity to have technical employment. There was an upcoming American Chemical Society meeting in Chicago which Dr. Lafferty would attend for recruiting purposes. It was arranged that Don would go and meet Dr. Lafferty. As a result Don was able to answer the need for a spectroscopy opening so the family moved to Oak Ridge. For a brief time, we all lived in our one-bedroom apartment. Since we had no car, there were a few times when we five would pack up and go to Cedar Bluff for a family outing in Don and Mary Jane's car.

Now Vickie was born in July of 1949 and two weeks later Johnnie and I and a whole bus load of vacationers took off for California on a two-week itinerary. We visited Carlsbad Caverns, the painted desert, Grand Canyon and even had "date" milk shakes at Indio, CA. We enjoyed many sites and places like Catalina Island, Knott's Berry Farm and for an extra fee most of the travelers gave up a "free" day to make a fast trip north to San Francisco for a bus travelers' tour of the city. The basic fare for the bus ride and the accommodations without food was $150 for each of us.

In the fall of 1949 we bought our first car, a two-door 1950 Studebaker. On leaving Oak Ridge we had to say good-by to our beloved Hertzel. We did this by giving him to a fellow classmate.

The man said to the mountain there

Why should I climb? Why do I care?

Studies at Oak Ridge and/or Knoxville toward an advanced degree reached a point where comprehensive exams were given by the University of Tennessee. Being away from academic life for 5-6 years and having no experience with Tennessee undergraduate studies were to my disadvantage and I failed the attempt to enter a doctorate program at the Univ. of Tennessee. Enter professor Dr. Hilton Smith who I felt saved my day. His suggestion was simple and that was to complete the requirements for a Master's degree and go somewhere else for my PhD degree. I needed a few courses in addition to a Master's thesis. I was able to work for the department head, Dr. Buehler for my thesis assignment. I left Carbide at the end of April 1950 in order to do my laboratory work that summer. Johnnie continued to work until the end of August.

My separation from Carbide deserves comment in that I was ready to retire but Dr. Lafferty could see it as a reduction in force since my services would no longer be needed. This change was monetarily to my advantage and included a free move to Champaign, Illinois whereas my original transfer as a single man was from Manhattan to Oak Ridge.

At the University of Illinois Johnnie found employment in the animal nutrition department where her first assignment was to dissect kernels of corn to separate parts for students to use in their animal studies. This was tedious work but as a technician she did it. We had a snowy time in November that year and one of her coworkers slipped and was fatally injured by a city bus. Fortune smiled on Johnnie in that she was given a job with the department during the rest of the time we were at Illinois. I took an exam my first year for an Atomic Energy Fellowship. I was ultimately declared as the recipient. During the second and third years at Illinois I received this Fellowship which had an allowance for married recipients. For my degree I worked under Dr. Reynold Fuson who was a brilliant and kind professor. To give you a sense of his abilities, I remember the time when returning from a lecture presentation in Italy he stated he had a problem. He said, "Now I have to translate my lecture into English."

18 - HOMES & WORK

Ready or not, a home to find
A tent or a cottage should we mind.

In the first eight plus years after my 1953 PhD degree I worked for DuPont at Jackson Lab, and Chambers Works, New Jersey and Antioch, California. We bought a home in Newark, Delaware and on being transferred to Antioch we sold and repurchased in Walnut Creek, California. On our transfer back to Delaware we had a home constructed in Sharpley on Halstead Road just off Concord Pike. A change of employment to Allied Chemical in Philadelphia, Pennsylvania precipitated a move to Moorestown, New Jersey where we were to live for forty years. Over all this time, Johnnie was never asked to seek employment outside the home. This was a family decision that she should be at home. On moving to Moorestown with son John who was now in first grade it was decided to drop the use of Johnnie to avoid confusion so my partner would now be called Uva.

When I was in my early forties, I was working at Allied and had a laboratory on the first floor and my desk was on the third floor. On occasions when near the top of the stairs I was a little short of breath. On using as little as 100 international units of Vitamin E the shortness of breath disappeared and has never returned. This precipitated the idea that most medical doctors had little or no nutritional training in the pursuit of their professions. I would try to the best of my ability to use some acts of prevention with regard to my health. I have used a vitamin regimen from that time to this for my family and me.

19 - PHILOPROGENITIVENESS

For unto us a child is given. Wow!
Now raise this one or two, but how?

John Sheldon was born on 8/8/55 and was treated as a pre-me but after surgery for a pyloric stenosis condition he gained weight normally. He suffered through childhood eczema. He was an active child who we decided would benefit from a second year in the first grade. He enjoyed Indian Guides and Boy Scouts. In Boy Scouts he progressed to Life Scout and had merit badges toward Eagle Scout which he did not gain. John worked part time as soon as he was sixteen and this later paid dividends in the Social Security system when he became qualified for Social Security Disability coverage.

Something went wrong in John's teenage years, when it was found that he had schizophrenic tendencies. Our blessing was that he was medically compliant. The whole family suffered but in time clozapine appeared. With the use of clozapine it was possible to stop all other medications. John's mental health has improved over the years if one does not look at too short an increment. Now at 50 years of age he is currently doing piecework three days a week, group meeting one day a week, and in addition is helpful around the home. In short, he is supporting himself and still has free time for watching TV, folding laundry, gathering trash and mowing the lawn.

John's condition over the years brought Uva and me to Mental Health support groups and I even served two terms on the Burlington County Mental Health Board. Our local group, NAMI FACE, was unique in that as a stand alone group we were able to advocate and we had varied successes in doing so. I served for one term as the president of FACE and was largely responsible for finding a lasting meeting place at the First Presbyterian Church in Moorestown. We would listen to tales of woe by newcomers and then the group would offer assistance in true support fashion. If you thought you had a problem then you should listen to someone hurting far worse than you. When asked one time why I was taking a training course my sincere answer was that I was there to be of help to others if I could. Others who participated include Lucille, Wes, Bob, Ken, Dolores, Eileen, Susan (the cookiemaker), Betty, Larry, Stan, Joan and many others. Here I apologize if your name is missing for I can see your face and the name did not appear.

Mental illness treatment may be broken down into five steps.(1) Diagnosis. This is not always easy but professionals do quite well. (2) Medication. Usually prescribed following a diagnosis. (3) Taking Medications. OK for the medically compliant, otherwise a problem may exist. Great patience must be exercised in looking for results. (4) Support Group. The patient or client gains considerably by knowing that he or she is not alone in fighting this illness. (5) Other Activity. Keeping in mind the frustration level of the client, he or she may undertake gainful activity. It is desirable to fill the time available so that the client feels self worth. NAMI FACE as a family support group provided the opportunity to learn of new developments, assist others, and to advocate for programmatic improvements.

Lisa Louise was born on 7/8/1959 and she was a joy from the start. By the time she was less than four we had moved to Moorestown so she grew up knowing this as her home. She loved working on projects with her mother. She tried ballet for a tutu or two. A summer playground finale found her on roller skates to the tune of "Hello Dolly." She became proficient in sewing and making clothes to wear under the guidance of her 4-H leader, Vivian Fix. She was active in youth activities at the church and she now does what Jim and Loudell Cole did with her, working with youth in church activities. In the summer of 1976, Lisa enjoyed six weeks in Iceland as part of an exchange program. She graduated from Moorestown High School in 1977 and elected to go to Randolph-Macon Woman's College. As a part of the program they offered the Junior year abroad for a selected few. Lisa participated in this program and as an interesting sidelight she was taking Spanish and in doing so went weekly to Oxford for her classes. In sports, she was on the all-English Universities' lacrosse team that went to Wales. I heard that Wales won the game. She enjoyed Christmas in a Scottish Castle and in the spring participated in a bicycle trip to Ireland. We were fortunate in being able to visit her during her spring break. We visited the Cotswolds, Bath, Salisbury Cathedral, Stonehenge and sites around London. The close fellowship of the Reading group facilitated Lisa's becoming class president in her senior year and an honored position in graduation ceremonies.

Now let us jump to another university, Lisa was to be found at Tulane for 1985-88 enrolled for MBA and masters in Public Health. On the occasion of her double graduation in 1988, we were there to meet John Roy Fisher when we enjoyed shrimp-etouffee that he prepared. John and Lisa were married 10/20/1990. We also met Cathy and her husband Tom as well as Marcia. It was on this occasion that I came up with the "ovel" idea. It seemed as though we were surrounded by love so maybe it just came naturally.

THE OVAL & THE CIRCLE

Let us play a game with letters and words. The word of interest is oval, if I can spell it.

O Obligation (commitment), Openness to ideas, thoughts and wishes of others.

V Vitality, Vigor

E Empathy (sharing with others), Emotion, Everlasting

L Lord, Lasting, Learning, Life

Whoops!, I misspelled oval, but look if I put "L" (Lord) first then I have LOVE. We are instructed that God is love (1 John 4:7-8). L for Lord, O for Obligation, V for Vitality and E for Empathy when put together spells LOVE. As God is perfect we can show love as a circle from L to E or from lasting to everlasting – no end. In following the Lord we are admonished to be like him. A Lord-centered life of learning with concerned obligation and vitality under empathy when all put together expresses LOVE. Our imperfect "ovels" (ovals) may never attain the perfection of the circle but we must pursue this goal with God's help and with LOVE.

Two years were to pass while John Fisher was in the Peace Corps teaching English in Niamey, Niger. Lisa went to visit which was a bit eventful on the way home because of an airline strike in Africa. She was stranded for a time in West Africa. Except for missing a few days of work all turned out well.

Lisa married John Roy Fisher on 10/20/1990. Their children Arman James Sheldon (b. 7/21/92) and Aigulia Uva Louise (b. 2/8/93) were adopted from an orphanage in Kachiri, near Pavlodar, Kazakhstan. It was December 25, 1997 when possession was transferred and after clearance in Moscow the Fishers Four landed at Dulles International Airport on 1/1/1998. Today finds Arman in sixth grade. He likes to run and wants to be on the cross country team. Aigulia is also in the sixth grade and one of her hobbies is working with llamas and she has many ribbons attesting to her showmanship. Arman is studying piano while Aigulia plays the trombone.

20 - MORE WORK

No work had I at first
But then rivers would burst.

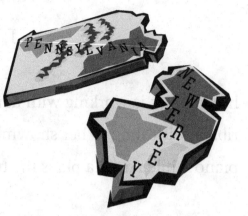

Hurricane Agnes wreaked some havoc in June 1972 in the Wilkes Barre area because of flooding of the Susquehanna river due to the heavy rains. As an employee of HUD (Housing and Urban Development) I was involved in assignment of campers as a temporary means for housing for those who qualified. When this job was completed, I went to work for Monroe Chemical Co. where we produced benzaldehyde and some benzyl alcohol as well as by-product hydrochloric acid. In the course of time, the firm was purchased by Kalama Chemical Co. and then in February 1980 the plant was closed. In April of that year we were able to visit Lisa at Reading, England during her junior year at cited above. That November Boyce Adams and James Palmer hired me to do computer work for which I had no experience. The project which we undertook was not financially rewarding so it was terminated. After a year of no gainful employment I started in January 1983 working at the Institute for Scientific Information. Their need for a chemist required abstracting key information from published journals to complete a weekly publication of new chemical compounds and a monthly publication of new chemical reactions. I enjoyed working for many "bosses" and included would be Pat Rosso, Dharmender Joshi and Shelly Rahman. I hesitate to list all my coworkers because if I miss one he or she would be offended and I would be in deep trouble. Love to you one and all.

When I was about to retire I came across the following quotation which it seems appropriate to give at this time. "We trained hard but it seemed that every time we were beginning to form up into a TEAM, we would be reorganized. I was to learn later in life that we tend to meet any new situation by reorganizing, and a wonderful method it can be for creating the illusion of progress while producing

confusion, inefficiency and demoralization." – Petronius
Arbiter (210 BC)

Adult studies at the Moorestown High School
allowed me to enroll a few times in woodworking shop. I
enjoyed making a blanket chest, two bedside stands, a book
case to sit on a storage cabinet and a harvest table. I
designed the table and did the critical work in the shop while
the final assembly was done at home.

Uva enrolled in an art class taught by Katherine
Ferg and she created a number of oil paintings which serve
to adorn our walls and add beauty to our home. She also
made a number of paintings on her own. At one time
macramé was very popular and she made a couple of very
attractive wall hangings at that time. As you can see she was
not only a technician in the laboratory but her abilities
included cooking, macramé, painting and as we will see, she
is expert in processing and handling dried flowers.

We both enjoyed growing orchids and participating in the Pineland Orchid Society. Uva also enjoyed the swim group since it was helpful for her arthritis.

21 - Some Church History

As we lived from day to day
We need the higher authority we say.

We came to Moorestown in January 1963 and we soon found ourselves in new membership classes in the Stockwell home. Among the others attending these meetings were Bob and Luci Rorke. We joined the Gay Nineties so named for the combined ages of the couples participating. Since many couples did not move to the 100-Plus club, it soon became known as the Friday Nighters which seemed more appropriate since we met on Fridays. One of the activities which the group sponsored was the annual Strawberry Festival with donated cakes and plenty of ice cream. One of the highlights of this event was the hulling session on Thursday night. My understanding was that the idea of this festival originated with Al Hodgen in the late 1950s. Later this event became a church-wide sponsored event. I can remember that our five cakes became three one year thanks to our dachshund.

The Friday Nighters included the Adams, Deroos, Fixs, Smiths, Pringles, Goodnows, Hambletons and many other couples who liked to meet once a month for the covered dish meal and an interesting program.

Ellis Derry was the scoutmaster for the Boy Scout troop which the church sponsored. I was on the adult committee and enjoyed many outings in which the troop participated. We had a brush with racial discrimination on the eastern shore of Maryland at a meal stop on returning from one trip. Barry Moore, an African American, and I shared this cold-shoulder treatment years later when he was an adult.

For a number of years I served as a representative of our church to the Moorestown Community of Churches. It was interesting at times to see the by-play of Canon Bruce Weatherly and Rev. Harold Myers. As pastors of two of the larger churches, they did not want one doing something without the approval of the other. For a few years the vacation bible school was sponsored by this group. While the Moorestown Community of Churches disbanded the regular meeting of the ministers of the churches continued.

As a member of session I usually attended Presbytery meetings. I enjoyed my time of service. Later I served on the Board of Deacons which was gratifying in that we were designated givers. Personally we found that tithing was not a mode of giving but a way of living. I enjoyed the joys of ushering, including the opening of the entrance door for attending worshippers.

As a part of adult education a class was held in which the bible was our lesson text and source. Rip Idler, Winnie Lyall, Joyce Peacock, Sheldon Frey and others served as teachers. The thing I remember well was that when it was my turn to teach it seemed that I would spend nearly 5 hours in preparation for one hour of class.

In the last few years, the highlight of the week was the Wednesday morning Bible class led by the pastor, Rev.

Jonathan Miller. I want to acknowledge the encouragement that Jonathan and Ken Eshelman gave to our son John relative to church attendance. It served well as a forerunner of his current church attendance.

22 - GARDENS ALIVE

Flowers here and there a growing
Now would they do for later showing?

I want to tell you of a hobby that I have enjoyed immensely and perhaps it may also be fulfilling to you. I enjoyed the beauty of natural plant materials and flowers in particular. I wanted to extend and preserve this natural beauty wherever possible. Some flowers are so fragile that they have limited use either for the arranger or the person owning the finished product. You can learn by experimentation and being surrounded with beautiful flowers in the process. These can be in a Williamsburg-type arrangement, or in grapevine basket as well as formed into wreaths to be wall hung or used as a candle wreath for your table. A whole world of floral art was opened to me and I want to share it with you. I want to thank my friends for sharing their knowledge and their gardens. I will also thank John, our son, for gardening work, Lisa, our daughter, for her creative work. I thank also my gardening partner, my loving husband for gardening work and many other details which made these projects successful.

Figure 54: Basket arrangement created by Uva

A GARDEN PRAYER

> *The kiss of the sun for pardon*
> *The song of the birds for mirth*

One is nearer God's heart in a garden

Than anywhere else on earth. ---

By Dorothy Frances Gurney

PLANNING

Now that you have decided to be surrounded by
flowers throughout the whole year you must decide which
flowers to grow in your garden. Do you want a garden of
many colors as in an old English garden? Now is the time to
grow many varieties of sizes and textures in a wide range of
colors. The decision is yours; plan to work with your very
favorite colors and textural scheme. To suit the occasion you
may need to consider formality and period. Consider special
pods for contrast in texture and grow something special for
holiday decorations. In the past I have chosen to grow
cotton that is unusual but a joy to nurture along. Grow
things that cannot be found at a garden center and have fun
doing it. Grow herbs for their fragrance and blossoms as
well as for spice wreaths and culinary uses. Keep in mind
that you may already have a wealth of materials in your own

backyard and not realize it. Certain types of leaves preserve well by glycerinizing. If you have a grape arbor, cuttings can be used to make baskets as well as herbal or floral wreaths. While a range of colors is desired, whites are also important.

SHAPE

Shape	Example
Round	Daisy and Zinnia
Cluster	Feverfew and Statice
Spikes	Larkspur, Artemisia and Golden Rod
Buds and Pods	Lily, Poppy, Nigella and Rose
Shrubs	Hydrangea
Leaves	Magnolia and Beech
Berries	Pepper Berries and Chinese Tallow Berries
Assorted Grains & Grasses	Wheat

PLANTING

It is wise to start seeds indoors under grow lights in early spring. I start cotton seeds soaking in water before I even start any of my other plants. The cotton seeds need to be soaked overnight to soften the hard seed and thus aid its germination. The planting media I use is a mixture of commercial planting mix, dampened sand and vermiculite.

After planting the seeds in clear small plastic flats, I cover the surface of the earth with shredded sphagnum moss to prevent damping off. The surface is sprayed with water and placed in a clear plastic bag. I place this container on a metal tray and on heating ducts to conduct bottom heat. I check for germination on the third day and every day until I see seedlings. Then I open the plastic bag and place the tray under grow lights so that there is about six inches between the light and the seedlings.

When the seedlings develop a second set of leaves they can be transferred to six packs or styrofoam cups. Remember that these young plants need to be planted in containers with proper drainage holes. Plants can be moved to a cold frame when the nighttime temperature is around 50 degrees F. When the ground has warmed after the last frost the plants can be moved to the garden. The last frost in Southern New Jersey is usually before the middle of May.

As the garden is being planted with home-grown seedlings I would look for supplies of plants and herbs which are more readily found at garden centers. Since these are ready for transplant they can be planted, too.

USEFUL FLOWERS & HERBS

Since the list is long it has been divided into groups receiving similar treatment. I have worked with all these materials and know that they are useable in floral arrangements and herbal wreaths. The art of all this is to know your herbs and flowers and to know what stage the flower color or foliage is best for preserving (see next section). If the specimen is too mature the petals may fall off and shatter. Some cuttings appear to go more to maturity after cutting. Some cuttings at maturity are at their prime while others should be cut in the bud stage for better longevity in preservation. Selected reading and a lot of practice in growing and drying of flowers and herbs can be rewarding by giving you much enjoyment. Since I speak of harvest times below let me point out I was living in Moorestown, New Jersey or about 10 miles east of Philadelphia, Pennsylvania.

PRESERVATION METHODS

A brief listing is given here of the various preservation methods which I have used.

Air Drying – Strip the cut flowers of leaves and hang in small bundles in a dark, dry and ventilated place.

Sand Drying – Place the cut flowers on dry playbox sand and then they are carefully buried with more sand and set aside uncovered in a warm place. After about 10-14 days the drying should be complete.

Silica Gel Drying – This method is similar to sand drying except that one uses a tightly covered container. Silica gel must have moisture removed after use by drying in an oven at 250 degrees F. for about 30 minutes or until the indicator crystals turn blue. Keep dry materials sealed to exclude moisture.

Glycerin Preservation – This is an old technique but it is rewarding when it can be used. When applied the leaves remain flexible, though they might lose some of their green color. It is well to do this on a hot dry time, in August perhaps. Do not place the foliage in water but carefully wipe the leaves clean. Split or pound the lower inch so that the bark and fiber are broken. Stand the specimens in a jar with a mixture of one part glycerin and two parts water. The imbibing of the liquid may be a week for oak or beech leaves but for southern magnolia the time required may be 4 – 5 weeks. The glycerin-water mixture may be reused by reheating and straining it. Some of the foliages which are favorites for this method include barberry, evergreen, beech, oak, juniper, rhododendron, southern magnolia and mountain laurel.

AIR DRYING

This section presents a series of tables summarizing when to air dry based on the type of material being air dried. The timing for air drying is true for growing seasons like that found in southern New Jersey. This section focuses on five different approaches:

1. Open flowers
2. Partially open seed pods

3. Formed seed pods
4. Fresh cut leafy stems
5. Purchased materials

Open flowers

Name	Timing for Drying
Achillea – Gold	Early summer
Achillea – Multi	All summer (use sand or silica gel)
Achillea – white	All summer
Chamomile, authemis	June, July
Celosia	August, September
Delphinium	June, July
Dock, rumex	May, June
Eryngium	July
Feverfew, chrys. Parthenium	June – September
Globe amaranth, gomphrena globe.	July – October (wire into calyx when picked)
Horehound, marrubirim	August, September
Hydrangea	September, October
Hyssop, hyssopus officinalis	August, September
Immortelle, xeranthemum	August, September
Lamb's ears, stachys	June-August (used fresh also)
Lavender, lavandula augustifolia	May
Lemon balm, aloysia triphylla	July, August (cut leafy stem)
Pennyroyal, mentha pulegium	August, September
Sage, salvia farinacea	July, August
Sage, pineapple	August, September
Sea lavender, limonium	September (dry upright)
Statice, limonium sinuatum	July - September
Tansy, tanacetum vulgare	August (use sand or silica gel)

Partially open seed pods

Name	Timing for Drying
Ammobium, alatum	July, August
Anaphalis	August, September
Golden rod, solidago	July, August
Verbena	June – August
Helichrysum, strawflower	July – September (wire into calyx freshly picked)
Iron weed	August, September
Joe Pye weed, eupatorium purpur.	August, September
Majoram, origanum	July, August
Mint, apple	July, August
Mint, orange	July, August
Oregano	July
Peony	June
Pussy willow	April (dry upright)
Verbena	June – August

Fully formed seed pods

Name	Timing for Drying
Basil, holy	August, September
Basil, opal	August, September
Basil, sweet	August, September
Burnet, sanguisorba	July
Candylily, pardancanda norucii	September, October
Chives, Chinese allicum	September, October (dry upright)
Clematis	July
Cotton	September, October
Dill, anethum	July
Fennel, foeniculum vulgare	July

177

Name	Timing for Drying
Jimson weed, datura stamonium	September, October (lay flat, seeds are very TOXIC – Psychedelic)
Job's tears, coix lacryma – jobi	August, September
Lunaria, rediviva	July
Nigella, love-in-a-mist	June
Physostigea	August
Rue, ruta	August (also cut leafy stem for glycerinizing)
Teasel	July, August (lay flat)

Fresh cut leafy stems

Name	Timing for Drying
Artemisia, silver king	August, September
Artemisia, southernwood	As available (use fresh)
Artemisia, wormwood	As available (use fresh)
Boxwood	As available (use fresh or glycerinize)
Dusty miller, senecio cineraria	September, October (lay flat)
Geranium, pelagonium	As available (use fresh)
Germander, feucrium	As available (use fresh)
Ivy, hedra helix	As available (use fresh or glycerinize)
Jasmine	As available (use fresh or glycerinize)
Juniper, juniperus communis	As available (use fresh with berries or glycerinize)
Laurus, sweet bay	As available (use fresh)
Lemon verbena, aloysia triphylla	August, September (use fresh)
Mahonia	As available (glycerinize)
Myrtle, myrtis communis	As available (use fresh)
Nepeta, catmint	May, June
Rosemary, officinalis	As available (use fresh)

Name	Timing for Drying
Sage, tricolor	August, September
Sage, purpurea	August, September
Sage, officinalis	August, September
Savory winter, satureja hortensus	October
Thyme	As available (use fresh)

Purchased materials

Name	Timing for Drying
Artemisia, silver king	July, August (tight bud, cut leafy stem, coil in basket)
Echinops, globe thistle	June, July (tight bud)
Eucalyptus, blue gum	As available
Eucalyptus, bloodwood	As available
Ground pine, lycopodium	As available, (hang dry cut leafy stem)
Gypsophilia, baby's breath	As available, (flower fully open)
Heather	As available, (flower bud partially open)
Monarda, bergamont	July (after petals have fallen)
Peppy berries, brazilian	As available
Statice, german	As available
Tallow berries, chinese	As available

HUMIDITY, HEAT & LIGHT

Air conditioning has given us relief from high humidity, but it is a fact of life that dried flowers, like crackers or pretzels, can reabsorb moisture. Experience will tell the more sensitive flowers. Spraying with a clear acrylic spray is a useful technique. I recommend storing large wreaths and Williamsburg arrangements in a carefully packed box within a plastic bag. Store them out of the way for the hottest months of July and August. After the hot spell has subsided the arrangements are unpacked and it is like Christmas. The arrangements are like new and are such welcome additions. When displaying a dried flower arrangement it is best to avoid high heat as well as strong light.

CONTAINERS & MECHANICS

Since any vessel has some potential as a container, it is most appropriate to have a unified product when the arrangement is complete. It is easier to start with a medium sized bowl or basket. I like to use silver or pewter Revere bowl, mugs, tea cups, rice bowls, small bean pots and popular antique kitchen items. What has just been said for bowls can be repeated for baskets: namely, there a wide variety from which to choose.

SUPPLIES

Other items you will need when working with dried flowers include wire, floral tape, glue, clear acrylic spray and oasis. I use 24 gauge wire. These items may be purchased from a garden center or a floral art store. Wire is used for extending or replacing stems. Glue is used to change or repair a particular specimen; for example, adding a petal to a daisy. Oasis is often glued to the liner of the container. Some containers call for a liner, which is often a plastic bowl that will sit inside the container. The tape is used to crisscross the top surface of the oasis and hold it secure. In the actual making of an arrangement, I use a small turn table so that I can rotate the work as I go along.

DESIGN, CONSTRUCTION & EVALUATION

There are a number of factors that enter the creative process, some of which result from trial and error. The artist must be as objective as possible about her work so that the effectiveness of design can be evaluated and improved. Important factors are considered below.

Figure 55: Dried flowers arranged in a cone or tree shape

Balance – Does the arrangement seem distributed equally? Since I work on a small turn table, I am able to keep checking on this point. If the arrangement is not intended to be symmetrical does the overall design follow complimentary lines?

Size – Size is an issue in itself. What is too small or too large? One and a half times the height of the container is a general guide line, but it must look right.

Texture – Are the varieties of materials in the arrangement complimentary? Is the overall product either too crowded, heavy or airy?

Figure 56: Arrangement in brass container

Color – Is color used well and to its advantage? Are the colors and shades varied enough as being complimentary? Are the materials well preserved, in good

183

condition and of consistent coloring? Do you use color to add depth or accent the arrangement?

Finishing – Is the rim of the container concealed? Is the oasis base visible through the arrangement? The mechanics of the arrangement can be effectively hidden by the use of filler such as hydrangea, golden rod, artemisia and pearly everlasting. You will find that softly muted colors blend together nicely.

WILLIAMSBURG ARRANGEMENT

I have used Sahara-oasis and ultra-foam and I find that they both work equally well. I cut my oasis to fit the container and shape with a knife. I use glue at the base and sides and tape across the top of the oasis. The top of the foam should extend about three fourths of an inch above the rim of the container. This makes it easy to add flowers at the rim to hide this feature. An exception occurs with the Williamsburg finger vase. For this container one uses a small brick of oasis wedged in each finger and supported by loose sand. The arrangement is completed using a complimentary group of flowers and filler as needed.

Figure 57: Artemisia Wreath

ARTEMISIA WREATH

The materials needed to construct an artemisia wreath include heavy wire (coat hanger size), straw, fine gauged spool wire, fishing line (15-20 lb.) and artemisia.

Shape the coat hanger into a 10-14 in circle. Then cover the wire with about one inch of straw. Wrap the straw with the fine gauged spool wire to secure it in place. This circular straw form is then covered with artemisia which is secured with fishing line. Artemisia can be used fresh or dry. I found it convenient to dry artemisia in a large peach basket so that it already had the shape of the arc needed to fit the wreath. Discard stems if out of proportion but utilize the end plumes to curl outside as well as inside to soften the circumference of the wreath.

The wreath is now ready to be covered with your flowers of choice. It makes for a more interesting design if one chooses three focal points such as 12, 4 or 8 o'clock positions in which to feature a theme which is repeated in the other positions. After the accent features have been added additional flowers may be placed in the open spaces. When each flower is added it is done so that the wire stem is hidden in the artemisia covering of the wreath. The wreath may further be highlighted by use of a ribbon if it is so desired.

GRAPEVINE WREATH

To make a grapevine wreath you need a quantity of grapevine. If the grapevine was cut fresh and stored for later use it should be coiled to approximate the shape you will need. If the grapevine is too dry and stiff, soaking it for a time in water will facilitate its being worked. While holding a piece of grapevine in the approximate arc to make the desired 10-14 inch wreath, start the second layer by weaving around the first and finally, you will find that a third pass may be all that is necessary to complete the basic wreath.

The guidelines for completing the wreath are similar to those for the artemisia wreath except that to show the structure and beauty of grapevine with its curling tentacles, far fewer floral additions will be used.

PRESSING FLOWERS

To press flowers one needs a press which is easily constructed of two pieces of half-inch plywood drilled near the outer edges to accept four square head screws equipped with winged nuts. The plywood may be 8-inch squares or circles. The press now needs only to be filled with cut pieces of paper on which the specimens to be pressed are placed. You may find that you will want more than one press. Collect all kinds of materials for pressing – flowers, leaves, ferns, grasses and tendrils. Many herbs lend themselves to pressing because of their color and interesting shapes. Some of my favorite items to press include artemisia, blue salvia, coral bells, dusty miller, hydrangea florets, Queen Anne's lace, buttercup, celosia, forget-me-not, golden rod, larkspur, lavender, zinnia petals and sea lavender. Press the items as perfect specimens and in various stages of growth. Press some full faced and others on a profile. Gather leaves or ferns to press in many positions. Pressing may take up to 3 weeks or more. In using the pressed material to make floral pictures use a good clear glue like Sobo or Elmers for mounting purposes.

POT POURRI

The word "Pot Pourri" means a medley or mix. In this case the name describes a blend of dried fragrant petals, flowers, aromatic herbs and seeds to which spices and essential oils are added. Some basic principles for a fine mix need to be considered.

Materials – Carefully dried materials are essential. Flowers must be gathered at the point of just opening to preserve the peak of essential oils and color.

Composition – Flowers typically found in pot pourri are those which are typically dried using sand or silica gel. To name a few: lavender, geranium leaves, sage, southern wood, sweet bay, tarragon, violets, bergamot, chamomile, rosemary, salvia, basil, lemon verbena, marigold, honeysuckle, thyme, nasturtium, rue, costmary, fever few, balm, peonies, roses, berries, tansy, mint, artemisia, hyssop, lovage, myrtle and heliotrope.

Seeds – Seeds of dill, anise, coriander and fennel are interesting additions to be made.

Fixative – Orris root is a fixative or an essential oil stabilizer and it has a mild violet scent.

Oils – Oils of rose, lavender, violet, jasmine and patchouli are available. Through trial and error you can determine the best fragrance for your purposes. For 2 quarts of flower mix I used one ounce of orris root to which six drops of lavender oil was added. The mixture was placed in a plastic bag and turned frequently for 4-6 weeks. Pot pourri is both a colorful array of petals and a natural air freshener. It can be effectively displayed in a brandywine vase, crystal dish or a ceramic dish so designed as to have air holes on the surface. You will have compliments for having this floral addition to your home.

TUSSIE MUSSIES

The tussie mussie is merely a collection of dried and fragrant flowers arranged so that it can be conveniently carried as a hand bouquet. These were used in earlier times in colonial parlors by the ladies. I have made these for wedding attendants as well as for Christmas tree decorations where a slightly smaller version was used. A still smaller version serves as an excellent final touch for a gift wrapped package for that special occasion.

RIBBONS & RECOGNITION

For this section I, the senior editor, will reply. Uva self taught herself this hobby which she thoroughly enjoyed and if you were to ask her she would deny that she is an expert.

The following are excerpts from page 8 of the News Chronicle Moorestown, May 26, 1977. "Paced by Mrs. Sheldon E. Frey with three blue ribbons in three different categories, the convention contingent of the Woman's Club of Moorestown (WCM) returned from the shore last week with 13 prizes, seven of them best in state. Mrs. Frey's triple triumph before 2000 conventioneers in Atlantic City came in artistic arrangements of various classifications in the Garden Department contests. We are particularly proud of Uva Frey, who batted 1,000 with 3 for 3, but we are pleased too with the contribution of all our women, not only those who made it all the way to state judging but all our talented artists and artisans who created our 33 winning entries on District Achievement Day."

"In Those Cotton Fields in New Jersey" was a 3-page article by freelance writer Jean Gaasch in the Pennsylvania Horticulture's publication of the Green Scene in March 1987. She gives the background of Uva Frey's interest in growing cotton together with great detail about its cultivation as she had experienced it over ten or more years of growing it. A number of color photographs show growing plants and their use in dried arrangements. One interesting feature which was part of the routine was the restraining of the bolls from opening completely by using netting such as old panty hose. The partially opened boll was much more attractive for use in dried arrangements. Suffice it to say that for medium and large arrangements the use of cotton became almost a signature for Uva Frey. Another art object from cotton was the empty calyx after the cotton was removed.

Figure 58: Uva Frey Featured in the Courier-Post 12/2/93

Cotton picking
Growing a bumper crop above the Mason-Dixon Line

Uva Frey harvests cotton bolls at her Moorestown home. Frey, who has been raising cotton for the past 10 years, uses the plant in all of its growth stages and even shares some with local third-graders.

Many shows and exhibits, while they were a lot of work, were both uplifting and rewarding. Uva made many, many arrangements on direct order by customers desiring her artistic work.

23 - RETIREMENT

Flowers here and there a growing
Now would they do for later showing?

VIRGINIA

Selling our home of forty years took a bit of courage but it happened less than a year after retirement. As planned we moved to Berryville, Virginia to share a new home with Lisa, John Roy and the grandchildren, Aigulia and Arman. All went well for about six months and then health problems loomed large and by January 2005 renal failure threw me in dialysis three days a week. We came to Virginia with three cats to join the four already here. Sweet William, Sweet Annie and Rosemary have since departed. Now to break the loss we are enjoying Baby Lou and Brother Thomas as they romp as only kittens do.

About once a week you could find me doing laundry. I usually fix breakfast for Uva and me but this morning we had a delicious one served by our grandson, Arman. We have enjoyed our flower room with the variety on geraniums, orchids, amaryllis and other plants. Uva and I find it difficult to be active gardeners since we move around with walkers these days. In Aigulia's 4-H club she works with llamas and we have enjoyed seeing her compete at shows. We watch some TV shows and I spend some time following my favorite stocks as the market goes up and down. We have been to the Senior Center a few times but currently we do not attend.

Lisa usually drives me for dialysis on Monday, Wednesday, and Friday and John Roy picks me up on his way home from work. The atmosphere at the DaVita facility is busy but friendly in spite of a considerable turnover of nurses and technicians. The treatment keeps my right arm more or less immobilized so I find myself either sleeping or watching TV.

Our church home is the First Presbyterian Church of Winchester. Our participation is now mainly limited to church attendance. John Frey usually goes to Sunday School along with the grandchildren. Lisa and Aigulia are active participants in the Sunday evening youth group. Much of this book I wrote while I was in rehab and now I hear requests for a compilation of some of my poetry.

REFERENCES

References are cited for the chapters to which they apply.

Chapter 1 – The Sullivan County Review, Dushore, PA, 6/9/2005 also From Wilderness to Wilderness: Celestia by D. Wayne Bender, The Sullivan Review, Dushore, PA, 1980.

Chapter 2 - Manuscript by Wayne and Scott Frey 3/21/1988.

Chapter 10 - Manuscript by Dolores Battin Troxell 10/29/1983 appended to a letter to Mr. & Mrs. Kenneth Frey. Sources cited include Kenneth Frey; Pennsylvania Archives, Pennsylvania County & Regional Histories by Collins Emerson; DAR, Biog. & Portrait Cyclopedia of Chester Co. by Winfred Garner; Index to Families & Persons by J. Smith Futhey & Gilbert Cope; History of Chester Co. by J. Smith Futhey & Gilbert Cope; Immigrants to America before 1750 by Virkees; Ingram's History of Sullivan Co.; Gen. & Personal Memoirs of Chester & Delaware Counties by Gilbert Cope; Gen. & Biographical Sketches by Futhey & Cope; U. S. Census; History of Sullivan Co. by George Streby, Swarthmore College, Chester Co. Historical Society; Twigs from Family Trees by Edward Hoagland; Pioneers & Patriotic Families of Bradford Co. by Heverly; The Battin Family Genealogy by Mouraine Hubler; Pennsylvania Archives & History in

Harrisburg, PA; Latter Day Saints records; Chester Co.
Court House; Sullivan Co. Historical Society; Mrs. Francis
Mulnix; Mrs. Mamie Randall; Mrs. Avie Williams; Mr. &
Mrs. Harold Battin; Mrs. Jessamine McCarty.

Chapter 10 - History of William Henry
Harrison, by Harriet E. Ridge, Lycoming Printing Co. Inc.
1969.

Chapter 10 – Underground Railroad - Hidden in Plain View
– A Secret Story of Quilts and the Underground Railroad by
Jacqueline L. Tobin and Raymond G. Dobard, PhD,
Anchor Books, Random House Inc. New York, NY 1999.

Chapter 10 - March by Geraldine Brooks, Viking Penguin,
New York, NY, 2004.

Chapter 10 – Underground Railroad in Pennsylvania by
William J. Switala, Stackpole Books, Mechanicsburg, PA,
2001.

Chapter 13 - There is an excellent photograph
of the family of John Floyd and Catherine Graham Gillespie
on page 50 of An Album of Tazewell County VA, by
Tazewell County
Historical Society, Pictorial Histories Publishing Co.,
Charleston, WV, 1989.

Chapter 14 - Annals of Tazewell Co. VA, John Newton Harmon, Sr. Vol. 1 (1922)Vol. 2 (1925), W. C. Hill Printing Co., Richmond, VA.
History of Tazewell Co. & Southwest VA, 1748-1920, Wm. C. Pendleton, 1920, W. C. Hill Printing Co., Richmond, VA.
The History of Middle New River Settlements & Contiguous Territory, David E. Johnston.
1906, Standard Printing & Publishing, Huntington, WV.

Chapter 14 - The Hornet's Nest, Jimmy Carter, Simon & Schuster Paperbacks, New York, NY, 2003.

Chapter 14 - Photograph of William Leander Graham (see chapter reference 13) page 7.

Chapter 18 – Vitamin E – Your Key to a Healthy Heart, ARC Books Inc., New York, NY, 1969.

Chapter 22 – An abbreviated list of references will be given here. Most of the references I have observed are good in this field so it is matter of choosing the book that has what you want.

Jane Pepper's Garden by Jane G. Pepper, Camino Books Inc., Philadelphia, PA, 1997. The Complete Flower Arranger by Amalie Adler Ascher, Simon and Schuster, New York, NY, 1974. The Dried-Flower Book – A Guide to Methods and Arrangements by Nita Cox Carico and Jane

Calvert Guynn, Doubleday & Co., Garden City, NY, 1962. Dried Flowers for all Seasons by Betty Wiita, Van Nostrand Reinhold Co. Inc., New York, NY, 1982. A Merry Christmas Herbal by Adelma Grenier Simmons, William Morrow & Co. Inc., New York, NY, 1968. Potpourris and Other Fragrant Delights by Jacqueline Heriteau, Penguin Books, Simon and Schuster, 1978. Potpourri, Incense and Other Fragrant Concoctions by Ann Tucker Fettner, Workman Publishing Co., New York, NY, 1977.

Clipart used with permission according to requirements established by MSN and PrintMaster 15.

AFTERWORD

There are some aspects of this book that deserve highlighting in retrospect. These highlights tie together some accounts which seem to be associated with one another or with historical events.

Indians – They entered the book at three points, first at an old campsite on the Frey family farm in a very passive sense. The second was used by my nephew in starting a family business based on Indian growing traditions. The third was more realistic with Levisa Smith Bowen and her African American companion in the protection of their stockade and home.

Underground Railroad and African Americans Levisa Bowen's companion is unnamed but she played her role and I am sure it was an uplift to her later. I recently had read "March" and remembered the references to abolitionists and the Underground Railroad. It was interesting then to find that Marshall Battin, my grandmother's grandfather and his sons played a role in this venture. I do remember my Father pointing out a lilac bush in the neighbor's pasture as being the location of Marshall's home. The use of quilts and other codes were not found in this brief coverage of the Underground Railroad.

Pioneers and Heroes – Can you picture a couple walking 30 miles to get married? Marshall Battin and his bride-to-be did. How are you about moving and/or living with danger? Moses and Rebecca Bowen came from Wales to Massachusetts in 1698 but then moved to Pennsylvania, Delaware, Maryland and finally Virginia. Moving into Indian populated areas was another challenge that faced Rees Bowen, grandson of Moses. He and Levisa were the second white family to move to Tazewell County Virginia where a stockade was built around the cabin. The account of Levisa's courage was cited above. In 1774, Tom Gillespie was cited as one of three men who turned the tide of the

Point Pleasant battle. Many "over the mountain" men made the journey to King's Mountain, SC and participated in the defeat of Maj. Ferguson and his men in 1780. An excellent coverage of this encounter is given by Jimmy Carter in the book "The Hornet's Nest." Rees Bowen lost his life in this battle but interestingly two of his daughters married into the earlier Gillespie families. Of course we would be amiss if we did not mention Col. William Leander Graham, a natural soldier, who played his role as a cavalry officer.

Printed in the United States
by Baker & Taylor Publisher Services

Printed in the United States
by Baker & Taylor Publisher Services